The Secret of
T⊕RGAU

The Secret of
T✠RGAU

Why the Plot
to Kill Hitler Failed

Jakob Kersten
and
James McMillan

Harrap London

Prussia is not a country that has an army. It is an army that has a country

Mirabeau, 1788

First published in Great Britain 1982
by HARRAP LIMITED
19-23 Ludgate Hill, London EC4M 7PD

© *Jakob Kersten/James McMillan* 1982

ISBN 0 245-53826-7

Designed by Robert Wheeler
Filmset by Martin's Printing Works Ltd, Berwick
Printed and bound in Great Britain
by Book Plan Ltd, Worcester

Contents

Illustrations

Prologue

Two men sat facing one another across a plain deal table. Outside the thick oak door two steel-helmeted soldiers stood on guard: one wearing the double-lightning flash of the SS; the other the folded-wings eagle of the Wehrmacht. No one was permitted to approach the room, let alone enter it. Under no circumstances — excepting only a direct order from the Führer — were the two men to be disturbed. No record was kept of the meeting. This account comes at second hand from General Oskar von Niedermayer, confidant of leading German generals: the secret man of the Wehrmacht who had organised anti-British activities in Persia and Afghanistan, supervised the training of the illegal German Army in Soviet Russia during the 1920s and early thirties, lectured in military strategy at the highest levels, returned to active command — and was secretly working for Stalin.

The two men in that room on a hot late July day in Berlin 1944 were the Chief of the German General Staff, Colonel-General Heinz Guderian, and the Nazi Party Deputy Führer, Martin Bormann. Their task was to cobble together an agreement between Party and Army to undo the damage inflicted by the bomb attempt on Adolf Hitler's life two days before: 20 July.

The scene was bizarre. Here was the most powerful German Army officer discussing terms with the second most powerful politician on how to compose their differences, while a few hundred kilometres away, in the west, the German armies were crumbling under Anglo-American attacks and a bare four hundred kilometres to the east the Russians were pouring through a huge gap in the German defences. The war was manifestly entering its last stages, yet these two men were not concerned with the present but with rewriting history for the sake of the future.

The craggy-faced Heinz Guderian was a German folk hero: 'Hurricane Heinz', the dashing, brilliantly successful Panzer commander, the apostle of armoured warfare and blitzkrieg, had led the Wehrmacht to triumph after triumph in Poland, France and Western Russia. Bronzed by the open air and still fairly trim, though stocky, Guderian belied his fifty-six years. He had physical courage in abundance, and neither did he lack moral valour in standing up to Hitler's more absurd demands. Indeed, he had been dismissed from his command for such insubordination, until military necessity forced his recall. Guderian was the very model of a modern Colonel-General: a professional to his fingertips, a theoretician of tank warfare and an outstanding battlefield practitioner; the master of the *Schwerpunkt*, the thrust of overwhelming might at the decisive point. Adolf Hitler and his National Socialist Party had been good to Heinz Guderian, providing him with the men and arms to realize his military theories and ambitions. And Guderian had been good for Nazi Germany: showing the world how revolutionary National Socialists could so charge the Prussian military machine with dash and élan that traditional foes like the French could be swept from the field in weeks. Guderian personified Nazi generalship, and in popular esteem was outstripped only by Field Marshal Erwin Rommel. But Guderian also embodied the prestige, honour and reputation of the German Officer Corps. As Chief of the General Staff — the very core of the German military tradition — he was especially conscious of his duty to posterity: to preserve that tradition untarnished. He was in effect, if not name, the emissary of a great power in its own right which had seen dynasties, governments and regimes come and go.

Across the table, in marked contrast to the fine bearing and impeccable appearance of Guderian, sat the podgy, low-browed Martin Bormann. With his close-set small eyes and jowly face, he was no one's idea of beauty, and a pretty poor advertisement for Aryan manhood. None the less, this far-from-prepossessing individual exercised immense influence over Adolf Hitler, Führer and supreme commander of the German Armed Services. For Bormann, apart from being deputy Führer, had control of the Party apparatus, and filtered all who sought contact with Hitler. He was indeed the Party, which along with the Army and the Security Service (Heinrich Himmler's province), sustained the State. The Führer's will was Bormann's law. At the same time he was intensely ambitious, and was far from ready to concede that the Third Reich was broken. The National Socialist state could endure, and it was his task to ensure that the Armed Forces continued to serve the Fürher and Fatherland until victory — or stalemate — was achieved, by which time Martin Bormann's authority would be vastly enhanced.

Thus both men, so different in background, appearance and careers, had the common aim of preventing a rift between the Armed Services and the Party and preserving unity at the expense of truth. Quite simply, ugly facts had to be buried in the national interest. And the ugliest of these was what had happened in Festung Zinna at Torgau-an-der-Elbe. The men there could have won Germany for the anti-Hitler conspirators and handed the Reich over to either the anti-Nazi government or to chaos and civil war. They had been forestalled, these experts in communication who, as Joseph Goebbels said, 'could have won if we hadn't been able to make some telephone calls'.[1] But knowledge of their treason could send a second terrible tremor through the tottering Reich.

It was bad enough that a few aged generals and disaffected elements should attempt the life of the Führer. It would be intolerable if it were to leak out that experts — not effete aristocrats and reactionaries — had also been involved in the conspiracy.

'Do you agree that we must bury Torgau?' Bormann asked Guderian.

'Undoubtedly,' replied the Chief of the General Staff. And so it was agreed by these two men to issue statements to convince Germany and the world that Army and Party were at one in the defence of the Reich.

Bormann's order, issued to all party chiefs on the morning of 24 July 1944, stated:

> It is the Führer's wish that in the treatment of the events of July 20, no one should allow himself to attack the Officer Corps, the Generals, the nobility of the Armed Forces as a body or to offer them insults. On the contrary, it must always be emphasized that those who took part in the putsch against the Führer were a definite and relatively small officers' clique . . . In any discussion on the attitude of the traitors' clique, the impeccable attitude of the Army and of the Wehrmacht[2] as a whole is to be stressed.

For his part, Guderian in an Order of the Day issued to the Army

---

[1]*Goebbels — The Man Next to Hitler,* — Rudolph Semmler.

[2]Combined armed services: Army, Navy, Air Force and Waffen SS.

on 23 July described the anti-Hitler plotters as:

> a few officers, some of them on the retired list, who had lost courage and out of cowardice and weakness, preferred the road to disgrace to the only road open to an honest soldier — the road of duty and honour. I pledge to the Führer and the German people the unity of the Generals, of the officer corps and of the men of the Army.

A day later the Nazi salute was introduced into all branches of the Armed Forces in place of the military salute 'as a sign of the Army's unshakeable allegiance to the Führer and the Party.'

Five days after that Guderian signed an order declaring that every General Staff officer must be a National Socialist officer-leader *(Führungsoffizier)* . . . 'and actively co-operate in the political indoctrination of the younger commanders in accordance with the tenets of the Führer.'

To ram home the message Guderian added these significant words: 'I expect every General Staff officer immediately to declare himself a convert or adherent to my views and to make an announcement to that effect in public. Anybody unable to do so should apply for his removal from the General Staff.' [General Order, July 29, 1944.]

The pact was sealed. The results delivered. And as both had agreed, Torgau and its secrets were expunged. But not quite. One witness remained — an insignificant Dutch engineer who had worked in Die Wasserkante, an anti-Nazi resistance movement with Oskar Ritter von Niedermayer, and who kept in his memory all that had happened in Torgau.

The conspiracy of the telephone wire could have succeeded if the anti-Hitler experts from Torgau had made it to Berlin.

But this book is concerned not just with Torgau and the plot to kill Hitler but with what it was like to struggle against the Nazis inside Germany. It is also an account of what Germans did to Germans under inhuman penal and military laws.

The forgotten men of Torgau are a grim reminder of what life would have been like for millions if the Nazis had won.

One

Seeds of Resistance

'Honour' is rooted deeply in the German soul. But what kind of honour?

Adolf Hitler described in *Mein Kampf* how he fell to his knees and wept tears of gratitude at the prospect of fighting in the German Army (even though he was an Austrian) at the outbreak of war in 1914. He regarded his four years' service in the trenches as a kind of holy sacrifice on the altar of his country. In the years of struggle to bring his National Socialist Party to power he kept at the forefront of his programme the restoration of the glory and prestige of the German Army. He made a fetish of wearing the Iron Cross upon a uniform of studied unadornment.

Hitler had a mystic adoration for the Army all right. But his army was not the same as that of the generals who looked upon 'their' army as a state within a state, while Hitler always saw it as an instrument of *his* State.

Yet both Hitler and General Hans von Seeckt, founder of the modern Reichswehr[1] and the militarists who followed his lead would have agreed with the words of Mirabeau. The German people existed to serve the Army.

Pride and arrogance strongly characterized this military élite: to an unbelievable extent in the pre-1914 German Army. For instance, it was a crime for a German officer *not* to punish a civilian who degraded or dishonoured the German uniform. In Essen in 1903 two former friends were home on leave. One, Haussen, was a lieutenant in the regular Navy; the other, Hartmann, was doing his compulsory military service as a private in

---

[1] Title of the small (100,000-strong) professional army which the victors permitted to Germany after defeating her in the First World War.

an artillery regiment. They met: Haussen in full naval uniform; Hartmann in civilian dress. Haussen ordered Private Hartmann to stand to attention. Hartmann refused; at which Haussen ran him through with his ceremonial sword. Hartmann died within minutes.

The officer caste was born to rule. That it was a caste may be seen from the fact that whole sections of the populace were excluded from officer school in the pre-1914 Army on the grounds of insufficient standing, and even in the 'democratic' period of the Weimar Republic 96 per cent of the 4,000 officers still conformed to that pattern. Indeed, one-in-five of the officers were of aristocratic birth, a slightly higher percentage than in the Kaiser's day!

They regarded themselves as the guardians of German honour in an unbroken golden thread from Frederick the Great through Scharnhorst and Gneisenau, Moltke and Schlieffen. Defeat, as in 1918, was to be regarded as but the spur to future victory.

Adolf Hitler and his Nazis endorsed these sentiments wholeheartedly. They too yearned to avenge the humiliations of Versailles; to wipe out the stain of surrender; to punish the 'November Criminals' (the unfortunate German politicians charged with seeking terms from the victorious Allies, thereby saving the German Army from odium). Hitler talked of the 'old cockade' and 'the old banners', and initially gave control to those who imagined a Nazi Government would restore the monarchy. But he had no love for the monarchy or the aristocracy. They had 'failed' Germany by not winning the war. The Aryan race was everything.

So while the generals thought they were using Hitler (Field Marshal Hindenberg, who as President presided over Hitler's installation as Chancellor, described him as 'a little Bohemian corporal'), Hitler used *them*. He advanced those who supported the Nazi creed, retarding or retiring those who openly opposed it, and all the time injecting into the Wehrmacht fanatical Nazis who thought in terms of a 'people's army', terms very different from the gentleman's army conceived by the generals.

The generals themselves were not as one. There were those who thoroughly approved of National Socialism — anti-Semitism and all. Others, the majority, went along with Hitler because he freed them from the shackles of Versailles, reintroduced conscription, remilitarized the Rhineland and gave them all the army they could possibly ask for. A tiny minority fought him the whole way — Erwin von Witzleben, Karl Heinrich von Stuelpnagel, Ludwig Beck, Kurt von Hammerstein, Erich Hoepner, Admiral Canaris — and (for a very different reason) Oskar von Niedermayer.

Even among those who could never accept the Nazi dogma, and who conspired against Hitler from the 1938 Czech crisis onward, there were serious divisions of policy: the basic one being 'Easterners' versus 'Westerners'.

From 1921 the Germans secretly trained the Russian Army in return for being allowed to use Soviet armaments and arms with which German soldiers could manoeuvre in Russia, free from prying Allied eyes, and in direct contraventionof the Versailles Treaty. Hammerstein and Niedermayer were two senior German officers who set up a German mission in Moscow at this time, and it may have been then that Niedermayer was converted to communism. He returned to Germany in 1933 when Hitler broke off the Russian connection.

Niedermayer — and others who joined them later — sought an alliance with Soviet Russia. This was an Eastern approach to the German dilemma of being in the centre of Europe, tugged both ways and subject to Bismarck's nightmare of a war on two fronts, while officers such as Witzleben and von Stuelpnagel resolutely opposed any deal with Bolshevik Russia, the hated Asian, the eternal foe.

Thus at the moment this narrative opens, in the spring of 1939, the undercurrents of rivalry were already seething below the surface of triumphant Nazi Germany.

Also under the surface was ideological resistance to National Socialism. One such organisation Die Wasserkante — the Waterfront — represented a segment of the Left-wing underground: a pitifully small fragment of a much-diminished movement.

It had grown out of opposition to military service in the First World War and it began in Frau Jansen's small flat in Berlin in 1915. Although the German Social Democrats in Parliament had voted war credits for the Kaiser, there were a number of party members who hated the war and worked to end it. First it was wives whose husbands had gone off to war against their will who gathered in the cluttered living-room. Then they were joined at these meetings by war widows, and each of these in turn gave refuge to Army deserters who were on the run.

Events took a particular political turn when the Bolsheviks seized power in Russia. The organization (it was not known as Die Wasserkante until later) then gave sanctuary to Russian prisoners of war who wished to join the Soviet revolutionaries. Frau Jansen's daughter Helena became Lenin's courier in Germany, making contact with Marxist sympathizers and others during the run-up to the German-Soviet peace treaty in March 1918. Then she and her comrades set about establishing the German Communist Party. It was after the fall of the Kaiser and the Second Reich's surrender to the Allies that the organization got the name Die Wasserkante from the Party's strong hold in the seaports of the Baltic. It was from these — notably Bremen — that it spread to neighbouring countries until by the mid-1930s it had twenty units, charged with undermining the Nazi state by sabotage and black propaganda — spreading defamatory tales of Nazi corruption and misdeeds. Among others it attracted to its ranks a young Dutchman whose personal reminiscences form an integral part of this book.

*   *   *

When I, Jakob Kersten, joined I was a mere lad of fourteen; thirsting for adventure, tall, tough, with already a rapturous sexual affair behind me.

Oh, I was advanced for my age all right. And a devil with it. In our sombre Zutphen home in Holland my mother was rarely out of bed and frequently in hospital. She had a terminal kidney disease. My distracted father could not cope with five lively brats, of which brood I was the least controllable. Always I wanted my own way. So at the age of nine the local authority put me under the tutelage of a Dr van der Borgh. He was my spiritual and temporal guardian, to whom I must report once a week and recount my miserable failings. He was also a stout communist and I was enrolled in the Red Club, De Roode Jeugd, the Dutch Socialist Youth movement. My mother would have approved — she taught me socialism when I was still sucking rusks. But neither politics nor the wise counselling of the good Doctor could prevail over my rebellious nature. At twelve it was the reform school near Arnhem for me.

Some reformation! I actually enjoyed it: football, gymnastics, rambling in the pine forests, bird-watching. It was quite easily the happiest time of my young life.

Mynheer Tims, our Youth Leader, the Iron Man, ruled us with a combination of the Bible and a bamboo stick. His assistant, Mynheer Moestdyk, made up for denying himself the cane with an excess of religious zeal. Yet there were compensations even among the youth leaders. There was Johanna.

Johanna was an athletic young woman of twenty-two, blonde and blue-eyed. I was a big lad of thirteen and a half. Johanna made the first move; indeed, the only one. One night she visited our dormitory for a final check. She paused at the foot of my bed.

'Koos [my nickname], I know you are awake,' she whispered. 'Don't wake the others. Come with me — I want to show you something.'

I followed her along the corridor to her room. The soft moonlight was just sufficient for me to see her face: her eyes were moist, her mouth pouting. She closed the door softly, and almost in the same movement put her arms round my neck. 'Koos, please kiss me . . . ' The dressing-gown slipped from her shoulders, and, naked, she led me to bed. That night I learned more about life than my books or tutors had taught me.

Johanna kept up the lessons, too. By the time I was fourteen I was extremely well-versed in love-making. My next art was to earn my daily bread. I was entered into the Zutphen Technical College to study electrical engineering with a view to becoming an engineering officer in the Holland-Amerika Line. And at this moment too I became an active, if very junior, member of Die Wasserkante.

Two

Niedermayer, the Red General

Without my knowledge I had been vetted by my 'aunt'[1] in Rotterdam, recommended by my guardian, Dr van der Borgh, and accepted into the organization by Gerardus Hartoch: all of them were in 1936 engaged in helping Jews to escape from Germany.

Hartoch arranged my first contact through the simple expedient of knocking me off my bicycle and drawing up in his old Ford car to apologize and offer me a lift (he bought me a new bicycle too!). He was an impressive man, well over six foot, with broad shoulders, a massive head covered in unruly grey hair and bright, piercing eyes beneath thick, bushy eyebrows. He had a large, hawk-like nose, a wide mouth and very bad teeth, which may explain why he smiled infrequently. Or perhaps his lined face betokened a life providing small reason for laughter. He was about fifty-eight. I stood in much awe of him.[2]

Unknown to me, Hartoch had chosen me as his ultimate successor, for he was getting too old for the game. He trained me in its details: as a courier to be unobtrusive, fitting into the landscape — which is exactly what a youth on a bicycle did in the Dutch countryside. Not that we had anything to fear from the Dutch authorities, but we were preparing for action in Germany, or in the war which we knew was coming and from which Holland could not remain immune. Hartoch also taught me self-

[1]She now lives in West Germany, and could be seriously embarrassed by a disclosure of her name.

[2]On 18 March, 1945 Gerardus Hartoch was executed by the German occupation forces in Zutphen for sheltering a member of a British aircrew whose plane had been shot down. A street in the town was named after him, and a monument was erected to commemorate him and eight other Dutch resisters who were liquidated.

defence: wrestling, ju-jitsu, and what became known to another generation as the karate chop. I was an eager and apt pupil. He was a demanding teacher.

My political indoctrination — I accepted the tenets of Marxism as a practising, if tepid, Christian believes in the Ten Commandments — came from the woman whom I always, even to this day, called 'aunt'. She it was who explained the purpose and outlook of the organization. Her experience went back to the First World War in Germany, and she revealed to me that from its earliest days Die Wasserkante had infiltrated German society in its highest echelons.

My 'aunt' was a dedicated militant; so was her friend Bertha Siebert, a wealthy socialist who befriended her when her husband was executed with the Kaiser's Army in Flanders in November 1914 (she never told me why). Bertha Siebert's fashionable home in Berlin's Kurfürstendamm became the secret meeting-place for high-ranking General Staff officers, professors and politicians, disillusioned with the war and seeking a Marxist solution. Her house was the upper-class equivalent of our lower-level headquarters. After the war, in the chaos of the early twenties, the two classes came together. They formed teams, men and women, sometimes married, sometimes just living together. Couples went abroad, often to universities, to found new cells.

'Aunt' I once asked, 'how large is our organization?'

'Nobody really knows,' she replied (and I too never found out). 'We are established throughout Northern Germany and we have recruits from Holland, Denmark and England. I remarried: a Dutchman, and came to live and carry on the organization's work in Holland. Martha, one of our number, married a Bavarian major and Doctor of Philosophy[1] who laid down a command structure which is with us to this day. It is based on the closed-cell principle. We know only the names and addresses of the ones to whom we convey the messages. The person who delivers it to us we do not know about. So if one is caught the link can be broken by eliminating the next in line. This, of course, only operates in Germany, where Nazis struck so ruthlessly and swiftly in their early days of power that we lost 80 per cent of our operatives in a few months. But the Nazis think they have caught only members

[1]Whom I later discovered was Oskar Ritter von Niedermayer. Ritter is the honorific for a knight: i.e., 'Sir Oscar' . . .

of the Rote Frontkampferbund.[1] They do not know, thank God, about Die Wasserkante and the closed-cell method, and we will see that they don't.' She paused. 'My son was one who was picked up by the Nazis. He will not be returning. 'But the fight goes on. The Major, now a Colonel, has ordered a rebuilding of the organization in Germany. We are specially concentrating on the intellectuals, and information is passed through one of our members — whose mother fetched and carried for Lenin — through Swiss contacts to Moscow.

'We started to plan years ago: carefully selecting young men and women from the Rote Jungsturm[2] and similar Left-wing societies in England, the Low Countries and Scandinavia. Many of them are "sleepers" who will be warned when they are needed. We are very like the Jesuits.' She smiled: 'Though you look more a farmer's boy than a priest.'

This slight, delicate, oval-faced woman had become a mother to me, yet she would as willingly have sacrificed me to the 'Cause' as she had her own son.

As I studied electrical engineering, so I improved on my secondary task of being a 'junior spy': how to move in silence; to see without being seen; to use shadows; to believe only half of what I heard, and not everything I saw.

Then one night Hartoch told me to report to Madame de Bruyn at eight o'clock. She lived in a large, rather gloomy house, Nieuwe Dam, approached through a lonely, leafy lane. Madame de Bruyn was an ageing eccentric, fanatically tidy, a local character — and a member of Die Wasserkante of many years' standing.

The maid showed me into the drawing-room, and there standing beside silver-haired Madame was a man in his fifties — a man of medium height, with a high forehead, aquiline nose and firm jaw, a man of high intelligence and forceful personality, a sceptic as well as an intellectual. He was also a soldier: Oskar von Niedermayer.

He started to question me. About my schooling; my electrical engineering; how many escaping Jews I'd met; my contacts with the (disbanded) German youth movement, Die Bunde, just 25 kilometres away from Zutphen across the border. Was I truly

---

[1]Red fighting front: a communist/socialist street-fighting alliance.
[2]Young Red stormtroopers.

prepared to commit myself voluntarily to resistance work in Germany? Did I realize the dangers, and was I prepared to carry out orders without question? I answered 'Yes' to every question.

'Very well,' said this man (I did not know his name then, or for years to come), 'you are ready.'

As I left the rambling red-brick house I decided to put my agent's training to the test. I could hear voices, so, collecting my bicycle, I stole into the undergrowth and waited. It was pitch-black behind the bushes, but the lane was lit by a watery moon. I recognized Hartoch and my 'aunt' and Dr van der Borgh and his companion, a factory-owner who drove the pride of Zutphen — an American Dodge automobile. Next came a couple who spoke French. Then two men from the other side of the lane who conversed in English. There was only one house at that end of the lane; it was named Huise Den Dam. The owner was a baronet; another upper-class socialist, a Böllinger Bolshevik as we called them.

There were perhaps fourteen people coming to meet the 'Professor' (I called him that, and he seemed content), just a section of Die Wasserkante dedicated — God help us — to the 'eradication of Hitlerism'.

Next week my orders came to conduct a quiet reconnaissance across the Rhine, to imbibe the atmosphere of Nazi Germany itself, to visit Düsseldorf during Carnival time. It was February 1939. I was just seventeen.

Three

The Police Connection

Small wonder Düsseldorf got the nickname 'Paris of the Ruhr'. It richly deserved to be called so. With its landscaped parks, traditional buildings and quaysides along the Rhine, Düsseldorf had a carefree elegance denied to most other German cities.

On this Sunday afternoon in late February 1939 the people of Düsseldorf were looking forward to another round of late-night entertainment in their annual Carnival week, referred to locally as 'The Week of Madness'.

It was a week in which everyone seemed to become obsessed with consuming large amounts of beer and food. The code was 'anything goes'.

This relic of the pagan past was also enjoyed by thousands of foreigners, who flocked across the borders from Belgium and Holland. They in their turn looked upon it as a week of friendship with their German neighbours.

My enjoyment of the jolly atmosphere was marred by the constant presence and never-ending marching of the SA, the Sturmabteilungen. Dressed in their unmistakable snuff-brown uniforms, Hitler's storm troopers — 'loving fathers of their people', as they were described in Dr Goebbels's propaganda — passed in strutting parade.

Using the clicking sound of their steel-tipped boots to step out the rhythm, the Brownshirts — bronzed faces stern under the visor of their képi-style caps — sang the Horst Wessel anthem.

Die Fahnen hoch, die Reihen dicht geschlossen, SA marschiert im ruhig festem Schritt.

and the menacing line

Bald flattern Hitlers Fahnen über alle Strassen.[1]

For me it was a spectacle of terror. But how different was the reaction of the spectators! These were the brown battalions who had saved Germany from communism, and whose relentless *tramp, tramp, tramp* — along with the tread of the Wehrmacht's tanks and half-tracks — had put Europe in dread. The Germans were euphoric. Within six short years of coming to power the Nazis had erased the shame of Versailles, brought Austria into the Reich, humbled France by regaining the Sudetenland from France's client state, Czechoslovakia, and forced England's Prime Minister, Neville Chamberlain, to come cap in hand to the Führer to secure peace.

For the Germans the jack-boots signified the triumph of the will. Small wonder that they raised their faces in ecstasy, and their arms in the Hitler salute.

After a while I grew tired of the noise and display and wandered along to the quayside of the Rhine. The white pleasure boats looked beautiful at their moorings, set like jewels under string upon string of coloured electric lights. They had been berthed here to give extra accommodation to the foreign visitors.

The paddle steamers especially had always fascinated me, and I walked slowly, examining each coat of arms carefully to see its town of origin.

The lapping of the river, partly covered with ice, against the boats broke through my thoughts, and I became aware that I was under observation.

Some fifty metres away I saw a lone figure standing partly hidden by the trunk of a tree. A woman.

The glare of the electric light reflecting on her showed she was wearing a black leather overcoat, not unlike the ones worn by the German police and known to most people as the 'Gestapo Coat'.

With these thoughts in mind I stared, and as I did so she began to walk towards me. She continued to close the gap between us with slow, definite strides, until she stood before me. I could see now that she was much younger than I had first thought; I guessed perhaps in her early twenties.

She was a well-proportioned, lissom figure, with clear, light-blue eyes set in a classical face, surrounded by shining blonde

---

[1]Banners raised aloft in firm formation. The SA march with steady, fateful tread . . . Soon Hitler's flags will fly over all streets.

hair tightly caught into two plaits behind her ears — it gave her a slightly puritanical look. During the few seconds she stood there her eyes seemed to scan every detail of me. Then suddenly she spoke — her voice was slightly husky. 'Are you looking for someone?' she asked me. 'Or can I help you in any way?' I did not answer her directly, looking at her with much curiosity. I tried to work out what a pretty woman, with such an authoritative voice, was doing here at this hour in evening, especially at Carnival time. I had been told to be careful with strangers.

I quickly dismissed my first thought — that she might be one of the riverside whores — because she had a very different air about her. Her ice-blue eyes stared at me enigmatically, clearly waiting for me to answer her queries.

I smiled politely, shaking my head in denial. 'No, Fräulein, I am not lost,' I replied. 'In fact, I like the boats and the sound of the river. The Carnival over there became too noisy for me.'

She smiled in return. 'To go by your accent,' she stated, 'I think you are Dutch.' I nodded in agreement. 'Yes, I am Dutch and live in Zutphen, not too far away from the border.'

At this moment she turned towards the boats. 'I too like boats and the river.' She emphasized the words, paused for a moment and then continued, 'Yes, the riverside is beautiful even in winter. The quietness appeals to me and I love to watch the peaceful flow of the water.'

She looked sideways at me, and with just a faint smile she asked, 'Are you alone, Dutchman, or have you come to the Carnival with a party?' I avoided a direct answer; instead I grinned and said, 'May I be permitted to introduce myself, Fräulein?'

She seemed surprised at this gambit, as though the formality had been unexpected. But before she could say anything I held out my hand and said as charmingly as I could, 'My name is Jakob Kersten.'

To my surprise she gently placed her hand in mine and smiled fully, showing off some nice white teeth. 'Welcome to Düsseldorf, Jakob,' she replied. 'My name is Inge Werner.' We shook hands gently but firmly, and neither of us seemed in a hurry to break the clasp.

'The pleasure is all mine,' Inge, I said. 'But what is a nice girl like you doing here alone on the quayside asking questions of a strange man?'

Inge laughed aloud, then raised her free hand to wag an admonishing finger at me. 'Don't be cheeky. I am here on duty watching fellows like you. I belong to the police.'

I released her hand and stepped back a little. 'You should not joke about such things,' I said. 'You may do so in Germany, but not in Holland.'

I could see that she was somehow startled by my reaction. She came a little nearer and placed her hand on my arm. 'I am sorry if I have upset you, but please believe me I am not one of the waterfront girls,' she answered. 'I am an officer in the German police and tonight I am here temporarily on duty. I considered it best to tell you this before you embarrassed us both by propositioning me.'[1]

I seemed to hear again the voices of my controllers, warning me: 'The Gestapo is everywhere, especially in those places you would least expect.' Her hand was still on my arm, and she returned my long gaze without a flicker, yet I could read nothing in her face. I must confess that I did not believe her, but I thought that if she were indeed in the police she must be in a junior position.

All right, the night was young, and if she wanted to pose as a police officer I was willing to play along with her, so I said, 'Very well, Sergeant . . . I plead guilty to being in need of care and protection.'

She glanced down at her wristwatch. 'I'm off duty in exactly five minutes. Then I shall get changed and we will join the Carnival. What do you think of that?' I nodded in complete agreement. I could not think of anything more exciting.

As we walked from the riverside to her flat we talked as if we had known each other all our lives. I explained to her that I was employed as an engineering draughtsman, and was attending the technical college studying to be a Merchant Navy engineer; a course paid for in full by the Holland-Amerika Line. While we talked I instinctively knew, with every passing moment, that we were each delighted by the other's company.

'You speak German like a native, but I like your Dutch accent,' she said suddenly. 'It is lovely to listen to.' I laughed in real surprise. 'That's all very well,' I replied, 'but what about *me* . . . aren't I lovely too?'

---

[1]She was in fact a civilian official; she had accepted a surveillance assignment for the extra busy time of the Carnival.

Inge shook her head slowly. 'You,' she said, 'are incorrigible!'

The late evening breeze, without the support of the sun, was now rather chilly; this was very noticeable as we crossed the Oberkasseler Bridge. Arriving on the other side, we turned left into Kaiser Wilhelm Ring.

The street was lined with maple and linden trees and overlooked the Rhine. The spacious houses had character, and were obviously expensive and well maintained. It was clearly a select residential suburb.

We had now arrived at the building where her flat was located. It was on a corner, and it was three storeys high.

Seeing the look of surprise on my face, Inge nudged my arm and said, 'Surprised? . . . Yes, rather posh, isn't it?'

I couldn't find the right words to reply, so instead shrugged my shoulders, admitting that I had been wrong about her. She seemed pleased by the gesture. 'Thanks for the apology, Dutchman.'

We entered the hallway. 'You wait here,' she said, 'I shall be a few moments,' and she disappeared up the stairs to her flat on the top floor.

As I waited I could smell the cleanness. I looked around me; it was rather a large hallway. On the floor were brown and white flagstones like marble. In one corner there were two large Gothic chairs, on either side of a small table. I sat down in one of these chairs, and noticed a large chandelier that hung overhead. It shimmered like crystal, and lit up the hall and the staircase, which was carpeted in brown. Across the hall and straight in front of me stood a bronze bust of Adolf Hitler.

Then my eyes fell on the name-plates. I walked quickly across the hall to look at them.

'Lord!' For there in black and white among the name-plates were ranks: Oberstleutnant, Kapitän zur See and Hauptmann. Then I looked at Inge's name. It read: 'Inge Werner. Chief-Secretary. Top floor.' I thought 'Secretary . . . of what?'

From that moment I decided to play safe and keep things on a very low key. Then I heard soft footsteps on the stairs behind me, and turned to see Inge coming down towards me. She looked beautiful. The dress she wore was blue, almost the colour of her eyes, closely fitted, showing off the curves of her slender body. She had undone the two plaits, and allowed her blonde hair to tumble freely about her shoulders.

Halfway down the stairs Inge paused for a second. I think she must have seen the look of admiration on my face. She almost ran down the last few steps, and stopping in front of me she said charmingly, 'How do I look? . . . Please tell me!'

'You look fine,' I said. At the same time I reached out, taking both her hands in mine and holding them slightly away from her body. I looked her up and down and our eyes met. 'You look so different from the girl I met on the riverside.'

I opened the hall door and we stepped outside into the darkness of the evening. The sky across the Rhine was ablaze with the reflections from lights in the festival centre. In the hours which followed she won my heart, and never lost it.

Four

Resurgent Germany

Within three months I was back in Düsseldorf. Hartoch called on me personally to tell me I was to go to a special meeting. We never put anything in writing; always it was by direct contact or by couriers — and I was to be introduced to a number of comrades as a courier for North Holland/Germany. I would know only their code names. They would know only mine: Karl.

I still recall the shiver of apprehension I felt when we crossed the German border. The very air seemed to breathe a purposeful menace. Everywhere were uniforms: the brown of the SA, the black and silver of the SS, the gold of party officials, the field-grey of the Wermacht and the sky-blue of the Luftwaffe. Even the civilians looked as though they would be happier in uniform. Their indifferent clothes (Germany was short of foreign currency, and was experimenting with ersatz materials) looked out of place.

Outside the station — cleaned up since the 'decadent democratic days' — I came across groups of Hitler Youth and Bund Deutscher Mädel — the girls' equivalent.

I smiled at an attractive twelve-year-old in white blouse, black tie and skirt. 'Guten Tag,' I ventured. She snapped her heels together, flung out her right hand. 'Heil Hitler' she shouted. I smiled no longer.

The station forecourt was like some weird, surrealist film-set with eight-year-olds shooting their arms forward at every second step to 'Heil' an acquaintance. You wanted to laugh. . . or cry. . . but you did neither. In the Germany of May 1939 you did not bring notice upon yourself if you were not 100 per cent for the regime. Foreigners were no exception.

Slowly I made my way to Altstadt, the old city where the houses were blackened from the fumes of the Thyssen chemical works.

I went to a house in Duisburg-Meiderich where I joined my 'aunt', then to the meeting which was held in the dingy, though surprisingly large, home of a lathe-turner who worked in the A.G. Weser shipyard in Bremen. He called himself Hans, and he took the chair as one after another we crowded into his living-room. I suppose in the end there were about forty of us. I was among the first to arrive, so I didn't see who was sitting behind me. To my left was an engineer from Frederikshavn in Denmark; to my right a fruit-stall woman from Gothenburg, Sweden, and beside her a charming girl — code-named Margarethe — from Rauma in Finland. We chatted quietly in a common language, German. Hans explained that I would be taking over from Gerardus Hartoch, and that my career in the Merchant Navy would be perfect cover for making contact with agents throughout the Baltic.

Suddenly the chattering ceased as Hans called us to order. He was standing beside the Oberst[1]-Professor. When I recognised the latter I stiffened, and sensed the atmosphere change. Here was our leader. Ironically, he belonged to the Junker caste, the barons and aristocrats, the warrior class to which Left-wingers were traditionally opposed. A voice behind me whispered, 'He may only be a colonel, but he is on the General Staff of the OKW[2], and is a close friend of most of the top generals.'

Colonel-Professor Niedermayer stood before us and started to speak. I made no notes. I would not have been permitted to do so — but his speech made such a profound impression on me that four decades later I can recall it in startling detail.

He began by reminding us of the events of the previous months: the absorption of Austria into the Third Reich; the surrender of Britain and France over the Sudetenland and the final elimination of Czechoslovakia from the map of Europe; the pogrom against the Jews; Hitler's triumphant entry into Prague and Memel; the opening propaganda shots against the Poles for oppressing the German minority in Poland, and for the unacceptable existence of the corridor separating East Prussia from the

[1]Colonel.

[2]Oberkommando der Wehrmacht: supreme command of the combined Armed Forces.

rest of Germany and the anomaly of Danzig, a German city under the rule of the League of Nations.

'Comrades' — and how strange to hear such an emotive word in the clipped tones of a senior officer — 'war is coming, very soon. Our foes are totally ruthless. I have seen these concentration camps. I myself was one of a group of officers who visited Oranienburg. Prisoners there are simply things, graded by coloured badges into categories — dissidents, politicals, racially undesirable, homosexuals — with a tattooed number but no name. Hours before we arrived three prisoners had been hanged by their wrists until they died. We viewed the bodies — unemotionally, of course, as befits German officers.

'Today there are seven other camps like Oranienburg. Tomorrow there will be a hundred. Some of our own people have perished there. Some of you may follow them.

'And do not say to yourself, "How can such cruelty be permitted to exist? Surely the people will revolt?" They will do nothing of the sort.

'Ninety per cent of Germans don't know what goes on inside these camps, and don't want to know. Even if they did, they would say, "Well, they deserve it: money-grubbing Jews and Bolsheviks and perverts — let them suffer. Adolf Hitler has given us work, purpose, fine new motorways, Volkswagens to drive on them and, above all, he has given us back our pride. *We*, the cowering, are now the masters. *We*, the common people from whom the Flanders front-line soldier Adolf Hitler emerged, are going to impose our will on lesser breeds."'

He held up his hand, then continued by telling us that the new type of leader coming forward in Nazi Germany would be different from the old. They would be politically educated in the doctrines of National Socialism. They would be revolutionaries. He admitted that members in the higher ranks of the Army had tried to resist them — from different motives — and had failed.

What was not known to us rank and file at this time (but was later revealed to me by von Niedermayer) was the Generals' Plot of September 1938. Fearful of a war involving Germany against a Franco-British-Russian coalition over Czechoslovakia, some generals — urged on by Ludwig Beck, former chief of the General Staff — planned to kidnap the Führer.

The Commander-in-Chief, Von Brauchitsch, was persuaded (much against his initial judgment) that it was his duty to frustrate the Führer. He even came to the conclusion that Hitler should be assassinated, thereby freeing the military from its oath — for how could you swear fealty to a dead Führer?

But the generals temporized. They looked to England to rescue them from their dilemma by starting a war, which the peace-loving British, headed by the peace-loving Neville Chamberlain, had no intention of doing. The plot came to nothing. Instead, Hitler got his triumph. The united front against Germany crumpled. There was no war. Hitler had been proved right again, and the anti-Nazi generals were discredited.

When von Niedermayer placed himself alongside the other Junker generals who opposed the National Socialists on class grounds, I wondered if he was perhaps using Die Wasserkante merely to promote his, and his caste's, own interests. I knew he had been in Russia as a representative of the army during the secret German rearmament of the twenties. He could have imbibed communism, or he could simply be following the classic Bismarck tradition of keeping the lines open. But then he cleared my mind of doubt.

'I believe', went on Niedermayer, 'that the destruction of the Third Reich and of the Prussian military caste will take place in the wide-open spaces of Russia. Here the alliance between Hitler and his General Staff will be broken. The Junkers will try to distance themselves from the forlorn Führer, but they will stand alone, having alienated themselves from their soldiers by the class barrier. Germany will remember their names as failures, stored away as an unwanted relic of history, and their slogan "By right of birth you shall rule" will be forgotten. It is our duty, comrades, to see that they never return.'

Well, that couldn't be clearer. And then von Niedermayer went on to emphasize that our duty lay with serving Soviet Russia. He made the point that the movement needed young men to fill the vacant places caused by comrades now serving in the ranks of the German Army, adding that our friends in Russia had asked us to help them in the gigantic struggle they knew was coming.[1]

He confirmed that the Elders of our organization had agreed and they were sure that war would begin in the autumn. Hitler had told his generals he wanted to test his fine new army in

[1]No one, of course, knew in May 1939 that in August Hitler and Stalin would conclude a non-aggression pact and agree on the partition of Poland between them.

blood.

'So, comrades,' he concluded, 'it is decided that from today we will act independently. Contact will be maintained only by couriers who will be introduced to you today.

'Any information, no matter how trivial it may seem to you, could be of immense value. It will be passed on safely to Russia.'

I discovered later that it was transmitted via the so-called Lucy Ring in Switzerland, headed by Rudolf Rössler and operating under the overall guidance of Alexander Rado, Soviet espionage chief in Switzerland, who was married to an Elder of Die Wasserkante.[1]

No applause greeted von Niedermayer as he sat down. After all, he had virtually conferred the death sentence on some of us.

Gradually the spell broke. We turned to talk to those sitting beside us or to swing round and chat with those immediately behind. I listened carefully, trying to absorb as much as possible. I almost ate the words that fell around me: names, places, industries, seaports, canals, what police forces to be wary of. I gobbled everything and digested it. I rose to stretch my legs, and prepared to meet others whom I was to serve as a courier. Then I froze. Not a dozen paces away was the girl who had not been out of my thoughts since we'd met three months ago — Inge Werner.

She was wearing a simple grey dress which seemed to highlight her stern yet strangely fragile Nordic beauty. Her face lightened at the sight of me, and she laughed, almost joyously: 'You didn't expect to see me here, did you, my young Dutch friend?'

For a moment blind panic seized me. She was in the police. Had I unwittingly led her to this secret meeting, and would she now proceed to blow a whistle and consign us all to a concentration camp? She read my thoughts and put a reassuring hand on my own: 'I am one of Die Wasserkante, with a lot more reason than you to be a member.'

At that moment Hans came up. 'Ah, Inge, this will be your courier; name of "Karl". (So that was to be my code-name!) You should get to know one another, for some time you could be working closely together.' He moved off.

Had Inge followed me that day three months ago, or was it just an incredible coincidence? I never did find out. I was too overcome by security-consciousness to ask then, and, well, too much

---

[1] See also *La guerre a été gagnée en Suisse* and *Handbook for Spies*, by Alexander Foote.

happened later.

Everywhere little groups were talking quietly but animatedly. Some had spilled into the hall. Inge took me by the hand and led me to a bedroom. My heart leapt. Half smilingly, she shook her head. 'Not this time, my lad. I need to tell you what I do, and why it is vital to the movement, and how I ever got into this in the first place.' This is Inge Werner's story as she told it to me that bright spring day in 1939.

She was born in Bremen in November 1916 — that made her five years older than me — the posthumous daughter of a German officer killed on the Western Front. Her mother was a beautiful girl, a dancer who entertained the patrons of waterfront bars. It was a crazy wartime romance which ended in tragedy — and Inge.

Her father's family, well-to-do and well connected in Leipzig, would have nothing to do with their low-born daughter-in-law, especially as she had the additional disadvantage of being born a bastard. So Inge and her mother made the best of things on a slender pension which, as the post-war hyper-inflation took hold, bought less and less, until it vanished altogether.

These were the days, in 1923, when you took your wages home in a barrow; when the value of the mark (2½ to the dollar in 1914) could fall from 1 million to the dollar to 1½ million in the time it took a tourist to drink a cup of coffee. So Inge's mother became a whore. She sold herself for food and clothes: for barter alone made sense.

Inge learned the uncompromising ways of the world in a sparsely furnished two-roomed flat in the Gropelinzer-Loidsstrasse part of the Bremen dockside. No girl ever had so many 'uncles' as Inge: a real international family; some cruel, some kind, some mean, some generous.

Inflation abated, economic normality returned, but Inge's mother continued her profession.

Then one day everything changed. An 'uncle' came who stayed. He genuinely seemed to love Inge and her mother. Inge called him 'Uncle Hein'. Uncle Hein was a communist. More, he was an international cell-organizer working for the Comintern organization in Moscow with the aim of fomenting revolution. Uncle Hein taught the impressionable little Inge her politics. He indoctrinated her, and because he was such a kind and considerate uncle she accepted his teachings.

But came a cold, early morning in October 1929. And as she recalled the events of ten years earlier her voice shook; she tore at a tiny handkerchief.

'It was just after 1 a.m. There was a terrible battering at the door, and the upper panel splintered. Then I was looking at two huge brownshirted men wearing blood-red armlets with the swastika. I couldn't even scream. I was simply paralysed with fear. I remember cowering back, lifting the coverlet to shield my head, but they ignored me and went straight for my mother and Uncle Hein, who slept in the same room, in a bed in the far corner.

'The leading storm-trooper brought his club down with crushing force, splitting Uncle Hein's head wide open. Blood spilled all over my mother. She flung up one arm to guard Hein and the other to protect herself. The second storm-trooper measured the distance as a lumberjack might. Then, taking one step back, brought the club down in a swishing arc.

'I heard my mother scream and I started to scream and scream and scream.

'Maybe I only imagined I could hear the blows rain down. All I know is that neighbours, who came to the house a lot later, said that their faces were unrecognizable. They were just pulp.

'Mother died a fortnight later in the Evangelische Diakonisen Hospital without regaining consciousness. I visited her and asked about Uncle Hein. No one told me anything. I am sure he died. And, of course, nobody did anything.[1]

'During my visits to the hospital a middle-aged woman befriended me. She was Oma Jansen, who had come to Bremen from Berlin at the same time as Uncle Hein, and had introduced him to my mother. I wanted to stay with Oma, but as I was only thirteen the local municipal officials were determined to put me in the care of relatives. In Germany everything must be just so. . . my grandfather was dead, but my father's cousin was tracked down in Leipzig.

'Ludwig Werner was a career policeman who had been a captain in the Kaiser's Army. He was a martinet without a spark of humanity, without any affection that I ever saw for his wife Annerle, and certainly none for me. He referred in my presence to my late mother as 'that Red whore'.

[1]The event was not unusual. In the run-up to German elections shortly afterwards 162 political murders took place in six weeks without any arrests.

He was a tremendous admirer of Hitler, and when he officially adopted me he had me enrolled in the BDM.[1]

'Of course, he had no idea that I had been infected with communism, and although he knew what had happened to my mother and Uncle Hein he didn't imagine for a second that that had driven hatred for the Nazis deep into my soul.

'I appeared to be a very good little Nazi, and by the time I was eighteen, after a year in the Labour Corps[2], I was considered ideal material for a secretarial job with police headquarters in Leipzig, and for promotion. After all, I had impeccable qualifications, with an adoptive father who was a captain in the police and a fanatical Nazi. So when the Geheime Staatspolizei (Gestapo) was being rapidly expanded I was asked to become a confidential senior secretary in Düsseldorf.

'That, my dear Karl, is how I came to be here now, and soon I hope to be transferred to Gestapo HQ in Bremen — where I can help the cause best.'

*   *   *

The political police had been set up by the democratic Weimar Republic to protect the State against extremists. The Nazis inherited the organisation, including its administrative head, Heinrich 'Gestapo' Müller — who was not even a member of the Nazi Party! The Gestapo was under the overall control of Heinrich Himmler, with Reinhard Heydrich exercising influence through the Sicherheitsdienst, the SD, a Nazi Party division which kept watch on everyone. On the outbreak of war all internal security was grouped into the Reich Main Security Office.

The key to State security, to keeping a check on everyone, was the system of *Strassenleiter*, blockwardens: persons responsible for their streets, blocks of flats, squares or perhaps factories. Each blockwarden was a veteran Party member who compiled a dossier on his neighbours or fellow-workers. There were probably 2,000,000 blockwardens in Germany at the height of the Third Reich.

Special attention was paid to the loyalty of the Armed Forces.

[1]Bund Deutscher Mädel

[2]Arbeitsdienst. Introduced by Hitler to train young Germans of all classes in the 'dignity of labour'. It was the intermediate stage between leaving school and compulsory military service. Young women usually served that year in domestic tasks. They did *not* do compulsory military service even during the war because that would have conflicted with the Nazi doctrine for women of *Kirche, Küche, Kinder* (church, kitchen, children).

In 1934 the generals had obliged Hitler to get rid of the revolutionary elements in the SA led by Ernst Roehm. In exchange for this the Army pledged its loyalty to the Führer:

> I swear by God this holy oath that with unconditional obedience I will serve Adolf Hitler, Leader of the German Reich and of the German people, Supreme Commander of all fighting forces and that I am ready to lay down my life for him at any time.

There was, however, still tension between the old-style Army chiefs and the leaders of the party's élite Schutzstaffel (Security Force), the SS. The SS chiefs did not trust the Army, and contrived to get rid of such generals as von Fritsch (on a false homosexual charge) and von Beck. The devotion of the Army was crucial to Nazi plans — hence the special surveillance on military men at home and abroad.

A special network of telephone numbers was established to provide direct lines for secret Party informers to get information on possible Army dissidents to local Gestapo headquarters. Anyone could be spied on — from private soldier to Field Marshal. The list of the members of the informer force was available only to forty confidential secretaries. Inge Werner was one.

She had proved so efficient — heading her special administrative course at the Prinz-Albrechtstrasse Gestapo headquarters — that she was congratulated by Müller and got to meet Heinrich Himmler himself. Then she went on to further studies: of geopolitics under Professor Haushofer in Berlin, who had developed the theme *Lebensraum* — living room for the superior German Volk at the expense of the inferior Slavs of Russia. The economic justification of the German thrust to the east derived from Haushofer's theories, and it is not too wild a surmise that Hitler's strategy in Russia owed much to his teachings.

Inge imbibed enough to impress her tutors and received further trust from her masters. She was appointed chief secretary of this special department in Düsseldorf, and was told in confidence that she would be advanced to regional secretaryship when older Gestapo officials took on tasks in the greater German Reich to come — that is to say, when the Germans moved into other countries.

*　　　　　*　　　　　*

One day in late September 1937 she decided to contact some of her old friends in Bremen, and she got in touch with Oma Jansen.

'She welcomed me like a long-lost daughter,' continued Inge. 'And in a way, she had become a mother to me. Odd, isn't it, that my whole attitude to life should be moulded by an uncle who wasn't an uncle and a woman whom I met more or less by accident?'

'Ah, Inge,' I replied, 'we are both orphans of the storm.'

She looked at me gravely. 'Don't joke Karl. The storm is coming.' Then she brushed away foreboding and continued in a lighter tone. 'Anyway, Oma introduced me to Hans and Maria, owners of an eating-place in dockland.

'They were pretty sure of me, but they kept sounding me out in the weeks between then and Christmas — I went to Bremen maybe half a dozen times during that period — and finally they brought me into Die Wasserkante, as a full member and perhaps their second best positioned operator.'

'Can you do anything for our people?' I asked.

'Yes, a little. I can delay passing on certain names to the Gestapo interrogating squad. A day's delay, a warning word from Hans and a berth on a ship leaving Germany for anywhere. Oh, it can be done. Occasionally. Perhaps one in a hundred might get away, and those only the ones I consider important. The rest go for 'political re-education' — a short life and a shorter haircut.

'But it's the Party's attitude to the Army that fascinates me, Karl. Most of the blockwarden stuff is tittle-tattle. Other secretaries usually handle it unless there is a real suspicion of treachery to the Reich, when it's passed on to me for onward transmission and I might be able to do something for our friends. The Army informers are different. I see all their reports. These soldiers of NSFO[1] are very smart. Of course, they are all on the make — the more accusations they can make stick, the greater their chances of promotion. They are advancing swiftly in the Wermacht now, much to the chagrin of the old regulars. But it's not just that. The party really is not sure of the loyalty of the Army chiefs — and we are about to have a war , Karl. You can feel it in my office. There's nothing now but talk of war; not if, but when. The party has sewn up the workers, the farmers, the bourgeois, the capitalists. There is not going to be any revolt from below. I

[1]Nazional-Sozialistische-Führung-Offizieren, Nazi leadership officers.

don't think Moscow believes that any more. Hans tells me the workers couldn't care less that there are no free trade unions. The Arbeitsfront[1] meets all their needs: wage negotiations, *Kraft durch Freude*[2], organized leisure. Who wants freedom when you can have a full belly and comradeship?

'The Army, however, is the sticking-point. Upper-class, tradition-bound, really despising Hitler, the parvenu. Everyone on the inside knows this: I see the reports. Yet the Gestapo does nothing. The party needs the Army leaders more than the Army needs the Party. If the Führer gives Germany victories nothing will happen. If there is catastrophe, all hell will break loose. The Army is the key, and that man,' — she pointed towards von Niedermayer — 'is our locksmith.'

I looked again at the man who was our undoubted leader. He was coming towards us. Clearly he had been searching us out.

'Well, Karl, so you pick the prettiest girl and take her to the bedroom.' I blushed. Inge rose. Strangely, she seemed flustered. She almost stood to attention. Then, mumbling her excuses, she left the room. Niedermayer — the Professor, as I always called him — laid his hands on my shoulders. 'Karl, do you understand everything that has been discussed today?'

'Yes, I think so, Professor,' I answered.

'I think so is not good enough. You must ask for further explanation for anything you don't really understand. That is vital. Not just for you. For all of us.'

He looked at me. 'Nobody here present can be sure he will survive the coming war. You younger members must be ready to rebuild the units and the cells. You must learn how to act in isolation. How to care for one another.'

'Professor. . . I understand that very well. I realize I have a lot to learn. Yet sometimes I feel a lot older than I am.'

'Life is the best tutor,' he replied. 'That is the reason we have chosen you to succeed Hartoch. Come, we must be going. We will leave in ones and twos to avoid suspicion. You can accompany me part of the way.'

We walked for a mile or so, mostly in silence. Then he stopped at the corner of Düsseldorfer-Nestorstrasse. He was going to leave me shortly.

[1]Workers' Front which replaced the individual trade unions and was an organ of the Nazi State.

[2]Strength through Joy. Holiday and sport.

'Professor,' I said hurriedly, 'would you permit me to ask you a personal question?'

'You know, Karl, our rules don't allow that sort of questioning for safety reasons.'

'But somehow I think I should ask,' I persisted. 'Is it true that, apart from your professorship, you are an Oberst on the General Staff and an old friend of Trotsky?'

His eyelids half closed. 'Where in God's name have you heard that?'

'Do not think me impudent,' I continued, 'but if I know that, so must others. You should be the first to take care.'

He smiled. 'I am grateful for your concern. Now I must leave you. The house I am about to enter is a safe address. Remember the number. You will be given a welcome and shelter at any time. The code is "Hans sends his greetings". The number is 62.'

'*Hals und Beinbruch*, Professor.' He waved acknowledgement of the old German good-luck message and disappeared inside.

From the Oberkassler bridge came the sound of tramping feet and youthful voices: the cadence of resurgent Germany on the march.

Five

Europe's New Order

It was the sound of the aeroplanes above Zutphen that told me the Germans had come to Holland. It is very odd to wake up and find your country has been occupied. Of course, we'd seen what had happened to Norway and Denmark the previous month. We knew that this time, in contrast with the Kaiser's war, we could not escape invasion — by one side or the other.

Hartoch had told me about a book, published in Germany before Hitler came to power, and called *Raum und Volk in Weltkrieg*, which explained that in the next war with Britain the Germans would simply have to have Holland as a base. They didn't have anything against us. We just happened to be in the way.

My first glimpse of the sinister coal-scuttle helmet and field-grey cloth was when a detachment in rubber boats started to cross the river Yssel in the bright May sunshine. That was 10 May. Two weeks later I would have been eighteen and liable to call-up. Instead I was a spectator of the poorly armed and utterly inexperienced Dutch soldiers trying to hold up Germany's storm battalions. We were crouched behind the Bult Kethe, like boys watching an illegal prize fight.

After a preliminary bombardment the Germans launched small rubber dinghies. The Dutch fire died away as the officer in command ordered his soldiers to retreat in the direction of Apeldoorn: except for one soldier who stayed where he was, on the bridge, and shot German after German. I discovered later that he was a half-caste from the West Indies, and the German commander was so impressed with his courage that he sent him home to his wife and children, who lived in Zutphen.

He certainly earned admiring whistles from my companions —
but so did the Germans. These young men around me were not
Nazis, but they had considerable fellow-feeling for the Germans,
and somehow they didn't feel part of the war. I did, because I had
been involved in resistance. They didn't because the Germans
were 'very like the Dutch', and military resistance to the Wehrmacht was 'hopeless'. Which it was. Within five days Holland
was overrun. Queen Wilhelmina and her family escaped to England. For the Dutch — so they thought — the war was over.

The German army behaved impeccably. They apologized for
the mistake in killing 814 people in the air raid on Rotterdam
(British propaganda claimed thirty thousand had perished), and
they went out of their way to be both unobtrusive and courteous,
especially to elderly people. They were like boys doing good
deeds daily. Because of our Aryan origin we were granted Reich
Commissar status, civilian as distinct from military government
. . . and placed under the care of Dr Seyss-Inquart, who had
been Hitler's man in Austria.

From the very first the Dutch Nazis, who I suppose at their
peak numbered 100,000 out of a population of 9,500,000, were
encouraged, but the other political parties — Liberal, Conserva-
tive, Catholic, Protestant — were permitted to function under an
umbrella organization, UNIE. But there was one important
exception — the Communist Party.

Hitler and Stalin had signed their pact and divided Poland
between them, but the Nazis knew they could not trust the Reds,
so from the start Die Wasserkante was on the alert; even though
our 'champions' in Moscow were fawning on our conquerors.

For the rest, the Dutch had no particular animus against the
Germans. Their presence was, of course, a nuisance. There was a
black-out. And food-rationing. But as the British blockaded the
Continent there would probably have been rationing anyway,
even if the Netherlands had remained neutral.

When the planes passed over on their way to bomb Britain
people would say, 'It's nothing to do with us. The war is England's business.' The Germans curried favour. They released all
the Dutch soldiers from prisoner-of-war camps, though they
held on to the officers and senior NCOs.

And yet as early as the winter of 1940 *Das Reich*, Dr Goebbels's
newspaper, was referring to the stubborn Dutch who say, 'If
England . . .' And so resistance began: almost imperceptibly, as

individuals heard of Jews and Dutch intellectuals disappearing, not arrested by the German army but seized in the night by the SD, the Security Service, acting on the advice of the Gestapo./

Before the war Jews had poured into Holland to escape the Nazi terror. Now the terror had caught up with them. The older Jews simply despaired, gave up and waited for the inevitable Gestapo summons. 'Look after the young,' they said. So we did. We got many of the young Jewish girls jobs as nurses in hospitals where they could be protected by the medical staff; mental hospitals were the best, for the Germans had a horror of mental illness and left these alone.

One such doctor to offer his hospitality thus was Dr van der Borgh.

He was outstanding in his generosity, and always ready and willing to help. So it was that I got my first resistance assignment: a mild introduction into that chill twilight world where the next moment could be your last. Really I was just a messenger boy, but when I recall the unslung rifle of the Wehrmacht soldier checking on identity cards and the cold, arrogant stare of the SS officer who made periodic visits to checkpoints, I still feel that being a mere messenger in an occupied country was hazardous beyond the imaginings of a middle-aged man. I was just nineteen.

It was Hartoch who gave me my orders. He called me to his home and handed me an envelope. 'You have to go to the address on the envelope and collect a woman and bring her to Dr van der Borgh at the hospital. This' — he tapped the envelope — 'contains her identity papers. Be quick about it.'

I glanced at the address. It was a house in Amsterdam. Naturally, Jewish refugees from Hitler made a beeline for Amsterdam. It had a big resident Jewish population (the diamond trade had not a little to do with that), and was cosmopolitan, so that a Jew didn't stand out as he might have done in another part of Holland. Jews provided sanctuary for other Jews, but in turn the Jews of Amsterdam sparked off a certain amount of anti-Semitism. Anton Musset's Dutch Nazis flourished there. I saw them as I walked from the railway station to the address on the envelope. Fresh-faced, good-looking youngsters for the most part, who looked on fascism as an ideology of the Great Outdoors, separating them from weedy, effeminate intellectuals, and, of course, from Jews and all other lesser breeds without the law.

It would be a mistake to imagine that Musset's organization

was composed entirely of bullies and what used to be known as 'hearties'. There was in these early days of the New Order in Europe, a heady combination of *machismo* and *Machtpolitik* about Germans and the Nazis. They were the virile ones: masterful and powerful, scorning the tremulous haverings of democracy, getting their way with mighty physical blows — and getting things done. It was they who built autobahns and Volkswagens and created full employment; they who raised up the valuable members of society, craftsmen, farmers, loyal workers; and they who cast down anyone who deviated from the normal. The Nazis could never have been so successful if they had not had a measure of appeal to basic human instincts, while the Dutch, like the Scandinavians, were the most favoured of the occupied populations.

So as I walked along the tree-lined Amsterdam street on that crisp October morning I paid particular attention to the muscular young men of the home-grown Nazi movement. They were to be found — for no particular reason, for they had no official standing under the Reich Government — at road junctions with legs akimbo, one hand clasping the brown belt, the other swinging loose, as though ready to draw a pistol.

I wasn't frightened of them: more angry at their calm assumption of authority over me and millions like me. The dread I had was that they might be permanent. For the New Order did not lack admirers, and at any rate, why spit against the wind? Why quarrel with the inevitable? Might is right — until overwhelmed by a greater might. I'd seen young men in brownshirts 'heiling' one another in Germany. Now they were doing it in Holland. And Belgium. And France. And Norway. And Poland. Today Germany . . . tomorrow the world. It wasn't impossible.

My first wartime 'mission' took no time at all with not an atom of risk nor breath of excitement. The Germans did not appear to have any cause to worry about the continued tranquillity of Holland, or the Dutch to fear the occupying power.

Sixteen days later we knew differently. Eighteen Dutchmen were executed for sabotaging the German war-effort. By 1941 the people of Holland were to realize that when the Nazis said they would wage total war they meant it.

The call to Bremen came in late 1940. It was Inge, of course, who had fixed it. From the start I was sure she had been determined for me to join her, not simply because of our relationship but because I was good, very good — cool, steady, reliable and fluent in German.

Hartoch, my tutor, reminded me of the ten rules of the game.

React to a person who uses your code. Use your code, *Hans lass dich grüssen*[1], discreetly so as not to attract attention. Speak to others as little as possible.

Never write anything down. Never keep any photos for fear of incrimination. (Inge had broken that one with her picture of her 'uncle'). Never forget an address.

Travel only when your controller says so, or when your contact requires you to. Always make sure your identification papers are perfect. If for some reason you are without documents, you must travel by foot under cover of darkness.

Do not carry excessive money on your person, and remember you are a foreign worker. Do not be conspicuous.

If your controller or contact orders you to go into hiding, never argue. Take cover where you are told.

Remember that prostitutes are the best underground operators. They have special opportunities to gain secret information. If a prostitute takes a fancy to you, play along with her. Your safety could one day depend on her reliability.

Should you happen to meet a member of your group or your contact pass him by as if he were a stranger. It may be that one of you is being followed. Never socialize with your controller (oh, Inge!). The exception to this is Hans, who is above the controller. Always do as he says.

Should a member be inquisitive he is a weak link and should be reported to your controller.

You must be able to remember ten different objects at a place. You must be able to recognize instantly faces and places.

Be on guard for individuals working for the Gestapo. They can be found in the most surprising roles.

Hartoch might have added an eleventh: 'Never lose the will to live.'

'When you get to Bremen,' he continued, 'do not on any account contact Hans or Inge Werner. They will come to you when they think it is fit and safe.

'I understand that Inge Werner will be your controller. Most

---

[1]Hans sends his greetings.

unusually, permission has been granted for you to form a couple.

'Here is your money. You will get your travel papers at the Labour Exchange this afternoon for the A.G. Weset shipbuilding firm in Bremen.

'One last word. Curb your temper. Other people's lives depend on you. Good luck.'

Two days later I left Zutphen. I was not alone. Thousands of Dutchmen, and Belgians and French, were taking work in Germany.

There was good money and social security there. Although Hitler had demobilized some of his troops following the conquest of France, there was still the air and naval war against England and (although we didn't know it then) the preparations for the attack on Russia. So while Germany was short of manpower, occupied Europe had manpower in abundance, thanks in part to the British blockade which kept the factories short of raw materials.

Bremen astounded me: the people, smartly dressed, alert and apparently good-humoured, the streets spotlessly clean, public transport abundant and running to time. If this was war the Germans were clearly enjoying it. Years later, I recall, they referred to this period as 'the happy time'.

Passers-by, tram conductresses, everyone from whom I asked the way, were courteous to a degree. 'Another Hollander . . . well, now, you take this road.' There was some bomb damage — sadly, flats near a hospital — but the site had been well cleared. Otherwise Bremen was as busy and bustling as in peace. The locals accepted foreigners with good grace, and the foreign workers, including French prisoners of war (one or two of whom had worked as PoWs in Bremen in the First World War) seemed quite content with their lot. If the British had realized how comfortably occupied Europe was accommodating the New Order they might have wondered if they would ever dislodge the Nazis.

For two weeks I worked in the shipyards, tuning engines for E-boats, and several times seeing Hans but ignoring him completely. Then, at the end of the third week, he came to me. I was totally in the clear: no suspicion, no surveillance. I was to report that night to the Essenkeller eating-house at the corner of Baumstrasse and Loidstrasse. I was not to go direct, but to visit the *Bierstube* next door, where I would be approached by the owner,

Frau Maria.

Quietly Hans described her, and continued, 'She will use only the code words *"Hans lass dich grüssen."* Then and only then will you know it is safe for you to attend the meeting.'

Precisely at 7.50 I entered the *Bierstube* and exactly as promised received the password from Frau Maria. Then I straightway entered the Essenkeller. The place was in semi-darkness. Only Inge and Hans were present: I embraced one and shook the other's hand.

Hans explained, 'We very rarely meet in any numbers and indeed even the ten members of a cell might not come across each other. Only two people from each cell know the identity of the courier who supports it. The less information you possess the less you can tell if captured.

'You will work for Inge and me. Inge will be your controller: she'll furnish you with money, travel documents, instructions. You may occasionally receive orders directly from me which will take precedence over everything else. That could include the elimination of one of our own members, for whatever reason.' He shrugged. 'Only in extreme cases, of course.'

'You may also, in an emergency, contact Frau Maria. She is a sleeper who has not involved herself in any actions against the State. In fact she is on rather good terms with the police. On Monday you will leave your present lodgings and take a room next door to the Essenkeller. New employment has also been arranged for you in the Merchant Navy. You are a qualified marine engineer?' I nodded. 'Your final role — and don't forget it — is to protect me. When you are not otherwise engaged you will be my bodyguard. Understood?' Again I nodded.

'Very well. Oh, one thing more. If you are captured take your own life at the earliest opportunity. We can supply cyanide. Or jump from a window. You won't withstand the torture. Clear?' He rose. 'I will see you again on Monday evening here at 8 to brief you for a trip to Mannheim. Inge will take care of your accommodation. *Hals und Beinbruch*, comrade.' With that he left. Inge and I waited for some moments and then walked into the next room where Frau Maria sat alone, keeping watch. We said 'Good evening' as we let ourselves out.

'This weekend we will have to ourselves — and we'll spend it in my flat.' Inge snuggled up to me.

'Are you sure that's a good idea? Is it a safe house?' Already I was talking the jargon of the underground.

'Certainly it is safe. It is owned by Oma Jansen, who has practically adopted me. She knew my mother. She knew Uncle Hein. I can pour my heart out to her. She understands.'

'So Oma Jansen is a long-standing member?'

'Of Die Wasserkante? She was one of those who founded it. She is one of the senior elders — and she gave her stamp of approval to your recruitment. You see, Bremen is at the heart of the Baltic operations, and it goes back to the end of the Kaiser's war when the Communist Party was formed in Germany. Today Bremen controls sleepers in Frederikshavn, Gothenberg, Hamburg, Rostock, Magdeburg, Mannheim and Rotterdam. We have a sleeper, Margarethe, in Finland, and the head controller is in Stockholm.'

'Margarethe.' I mused. 'Oma Jansen, yourself. Why are there so many women in the organization?'

'Quite simple. The organization started as a link for anti-war deserters in the First World War. Women — elderly now — provided the safe havens. Recently many men have been arrested as the Gestapo has closed in on the Communist Party activists. Sisters, daughters, girlfriends have taken over.'

We made love on and off for the whole weekend. It was wonderful, even if it was not war!

Six

Sabotage and Execution

The Left-wing resistance to Hitler really came into its own when Germany invaded Russia on 22 June 1941. Until then the Nazis had hunted down communists in the occupied territories as part of the general campaign against 'dissident and sub-human types' — Jews, gipsies, the mentally infirm, homosexuals as well as Reds. The Hitler-Stalin pact — which by giving Germany a free hand in Poland was an immediate cause of the war — in no way inhibited the Sicherheitsdienst (the security arm of the SS) from ridding the New Europe of unacceptable elements. In turn we Reds hit back: more out of an automatic response, having fought the Nazis so long, than from deliberate policy.

It is strange, looking back, to remember how readily Europe bowed to the dominance of Germany. Resistance in these early days — and it was mainly from patriotic individuals, ex-officers and the like — amounted to the merest pin-pricks.

A favoured Wasserkante device was to send trains carrying troops and munitions to the wrong destination. We had to be very careful about this, to avoid betraying our own men in the railway service. The destination dockets, forged by our experts, sent freight to the north instead of the south; the west instead of the east. During the short Balkan campaign in April 1941 we successfully diverted some shipments that way. And always our impeccable railway servant had a perfect German answer. 'But, Herr Inspector, here are the documents. If they are not the genuine ones, how was I to know? Someone else has blundered. I obeyed orders. Invariably I obey orders, Herr Inspector.'

Naturally the Reich Railways perfected a check-back system which brought an end to that little game; and game it was, despite the risks run.

Everything changed the moment the Panzers crashed through the Soviet frontier. Now the war became a crusade: pitting buoyant, youthful, hopeful communism against soulless, evil fascism. We believed in Stalin in the way early Christians did in St Paul.

So my excitement was intense when Hans alerted me to my first sabotage assignment.

From our senior agent in Stockholm we learned that the German-Finnish command were preparing an autumn offensive to take Murmansk, the Arctic port through which British and American munitions and supplies reached Russia.

The only reliable form of transport in that trackless waste was reindeer and pony. So thousands of tons of straw were needed for the animals' bedding and feeding. General Rossi, commanding the German-Finnish force at Petsamo, the Finnish port nearest Murmansk, was adamant that without adequate feeding-stock there was no hope of sustaining the assault. We knew Rossi's view because Niedermayer was an old friend of numerous senior officers at OKW, who naturally spoke openly to him of coming operations.

At that time — August 1941 — Niedermayer was professor of geopolitics at Berlin University, but expecting to be recalled to the colours (he had retired on half-pay a couple of years previously), and in daily touch with the Wehrmacht's leading personalities.

We thus had double confirmation that frustrating Operation Straw would deal a decisive blow at one vital junction of the Eastern Front. For if the Germans took Murmansk they would rob the Western allies of their principal line of communication with the Soviet Union. And if the Germans didn't take Murmansk in the autumn, winter weather would render the operation impossible, and by the summer of 1942 the port could be made impregnable.

The key to Operation Straw was the steamship *Herrenwyck*, loading at Wismar on the Baltic en route for Petsamo. Group Bremen was ordered to stop it, regardless of cost.

Few in numbers though we were, we had penetrated the German Baltic at certain crucial points. We had one or two sympathetic agents who appointed crews for specific assignments. The trip to Petsamo, up the Norwegian coastline, was not a popular one. Ships were liable to be bombed by the RAF or torpedoed by the Royal Navy. So we had, without too much difficulty, succeeded in getting one of our men, Herr Hillman, on the *Herrenwyck* as chief engineer. My task was to join him as assistant engineer, and to this end I presented myself to the shipping line's representative in Bremen. All went smoothly, and I boarded the *Herrenwyck* and went in search of Herr Hillman.

It was odd, but at the time you felt you could instinctively recognise anti-Nazis from their fresh, manly gaze and understanding eyes. Nonsense, of course. I was to meet Nazis who seemed perfectly normal, even likeable, and resisters who were positively reptilian. But at this juncture I was still full of boyish idealism.

Chief Engineer Hillman offered me his bed as I spoke the code words: *Hans lass dich grüssen.* He was a strongly built, grey-haired man of about sixty, and his grip was true and comradely. He checked my papers minutely. 'You take no chances,' I observed. 'Not in this game, comrade,' he replied. How the old fighters loved the word comrade.

We sat in his carpeted, comfortable cabin and discussed tactics, very quietly and with one eye on the door, for though most of the crew were politically disinterested, the first mate was a fanatical Nazi who listened to everyone's conversation.

'There will be three of us to man the engine-room,' said Hillman. 'The third engineer is a good enough fellow but not very bright. The plan is simple: we jam the steering to run her on to a sandbank. She's an 8,000-tonner, and the damage will be considerable. She might even ship water. Anyway, she'll need a tow and considerable repairs. The consignment could be delayed by weeks and weeks.'

'Won't deliberate jamming be spotted at the repair dock?'

'Possibly, but we'll have to take the chance they won't be looking for sabotage. We operate four hours on and eight off. I'll make sure we do two consecutive stints, so that'll give us eight hours to fix the steering at the right point.'

I nodded, rose and walked out into the passageway. My stomach turned a somersault when I discovered the first mate only a few paces away. Had he overheard? I was never gifted — or cursed — with imagination, but I none the less felt mounting fear as he approached me. I stared at the little gold and red Party badge on his uniform. 'Hullo, Hollander,' he grinned. 'Welcome aboard.'

Not for the last time, I was to learn that when you fear most you have nothing to fear. The blow comes when it is least expected.

Captain Dzeder, a broadly built, grizzled sailor, had sailed the Baltic, and most other seas, for thirty years. A thorough going professional, he estimated the odds of getting to Petsamo at no more than fifty-fifty.

'So long as we are in the Baltic we have to look out for natural hazards. The British will bomb the ports at night, but during the day we enjoy excellent cover, not only from our own batteries and the Luftwaffe but also from the Swedes. They are very punctilious about defending their air-space and they have a generous estimate of how far that extends. Sweden is a most useful neutral.[1]

'Outside the Baltic we have the still more treacherous Norwegian coast, and single ships like ours make a tempting target for enemy bombers, submarines or roving surface raiders.'

I thought: 'And there is another hazard you cannot even imagine.'

The second morning out the weather changed from fine to a rain-spattering gale. Hillman had not yet arranged the time and position for sabotaging the steering gear. I was due on duty at midday. A few minutes after eleven o'clock I noticed there was something wrong with the engine. Suddenly, jarringly, the ship stopped. I heard footsteps — boots thumping on the deck. I pulled myself off my bunk, donned my trousers and raced on deck. The *Herrenwyck* had run aground on a sandbank! A navigational blunder, a miscalculation from the bridge, had done the job for us.

Nearly thirty-six hours passed before tugs pulled us off, and then we started to ship water. We were ordered to Rostock to unload and to undergo repairs. With the time it would take to unload and find another ship the Germans' opportunity at Murmansk would have gone.

General Rossi never received his straw. The attack on Murmansk was never mounted — and the Bremen Group and young Kersten in particular got wholly undeserved credit for sabotaging a ship that suffered a straightforward accident. Such is the irony of war.

With the *Herrenwyck* tied up for two weeks I was anxious to get

[1]Sweden also permitted German troops to cross from conquered Norway to Finland to support the Finns fighting Russia.

on with my next assignment. Hillman arranged that I should go ashore for more than twelve hours so that the Chief would have an excuse to dismiss me.

I slipped off and took refuge with a Wasserkante sleeper, Magda, who operated as a prostitute near dockland.

Magda was a fine-looking female: long black, sleek hair, large brown eyes, olive complexion, slender and sensuous. If I hadn't been in love with blonde, Nordic Inge, I could have really fallen for her.

I stayed the night with Magda and returned to the *Herrenwyck*, from which I was instantly dismissed, but with a letter from Chief Hillman excusing my conduct on the grounds of lusty youth (at this juncture the German Merchant Navy was *not* under military control).

So I jauntily descended the gangplank, small, battered fibre suitcase in hand, only to be met by a man wearing a long black raincoat who clapped me on the shoulder.

'Are you Kersten?'

'Yes, why?'

'You are under arrest. Come with me to the police station.'

At the station I was put into a cell and told to await the arrival of an interrogation officer. I sat on the bench bed thinking dread thoughts of 're-education camps' (this is how concentration camps were described).

Suddenly the door burst open and the muscular Gestapo man who had carried out the arrest rushed at me like a mad bull. I learned later that this was their favourite method of shattering suspects. He grabbed hold of me by the collar and swung his right fist into my eye. That was followed by another blow, and another. I fell to the floor. He stood back to allow me to pick myself up and rub the blood from my face.

'That's for leaving your post without permission,' he screamed. 'You know it is an offence not to report your movements. But your first mate reported your disobedience.'

Question followed question. Non-stop: 'Who are you? Where are you going? When did you get your papers? What was your mother's maiden name? How many in the family? Where have you been since yesterday evening?' Designed to confuse and trap you into a fatal admission.

I told him about Magda. 'I slept with a whore last night and overslept this morning.'

My interrogator turned on his heels and left me nursing my swelling eyes. Within minutes he was back, and Magda with him. She stared hard to make sure it was me, and then corroborated my story in a thoroughly convincing manner. Without further ado I was released, after signing a statement that I had not been ill treated.

Magda took me to her home bathed my bruises and provided further loving care in bed. As we lay, cradled in each other's arms, I surveyed the trials and frustrations of resistance. A success, through accident, and a Gestapo roughing-up that had nothing whatsoever to do with my fight against Hitler. I turned on my side — and Magda turned on hers.

The months slipped by. We tried another bit of Baltic shipping sabotage. This concerned an ore-carrying vessel, the *Frielinghaus*. She plied regularly from Sweden to Rotterdam, carrying high-grade Swedish ore for the Ruhr arms factories. Blowing a hole in the *Frielinghaus* would cause minimal upset to the German war machine, but disabling her in a strategic position, such as the mouth of the Rhine or in the Kiel Canal, could wreck Baltic shipping schedules. So it was decided that I should join with an explosives expert called Mucke from the Hamburg group to fix the *Frielinghaus*, which was docked at Hamburg. I got myself enrolled as a crew member so that I could come and go without question. Mucke was recognized as my friend. And so it was that while I distracted the watch he nipped along to the engine-room to plant the device. Seven minutes were allowed for attaching the explosive and setting a delayed-action fuse — fixed to go off when the ship was in the Kiel Canal.

I kept the conversation going for ten. Then out of the corner of my eye I saw Mucke emerge, giving the thumbs up sign. I diverted the guard's attention while he sneaked down the gangway. Shortly afterwards I made my excuses about enjoying a woman for the night and disappeared too.

The *Frielinghaus* sailed on schedule. Unfortunately for the plans of the Resistance, the device exploded far earlier than had been calculated. She blew up and sank off Northerney, posing no obstruction whatever to shipping. The timing had been faulty. Hans was not amused. But it was not Hans I had to worry about.

I was sitting relaxing in Inge's apartment in Bremen when the door opened, framing Oma Jansen. She no longer looked a benign old dear. The silver hair topped grim, cold features. She motioned me to follow her into her room.

Reluctantly, with a show of bravado I did not feel, I rose languidly, hands in pockets.

'*Schnell!*' The word spat out like a bullet. I obeyed instantly, crossing the intervening space at the double, and stood at attention. At that moment I realized that Oma Jansen was the real head of Die Wasserkante: the Elder of Elders, to whom even Oskar Ritter von Niedermayer, had to defer.

I did not confirm that impression until years later, but instinctively I knew then that this elderly woman (she must have been in her late sixties), who had espoused Marxism from the turn of the century, had befriended Lenin in his days of exile, and had agitated for revolution during the Kaiser's war, was the driving force of Die Wasserkante.

She sat down on a hard-backed chair behind a table. She made no move to offer me a seat. I remained rigid.

'Now understand this, Kersten, you and Mucke failed with the *Frielinghaus.*'

'I am not an explosives expert.'

'Keep silent when I am speaking, comrade. You should both have checked the timing device. Carelessness in future will not go unpunished. You've been lucky. You've never been in danger.'

This time I interrupted hotly, 'but I want danger. I want to kill Germans.'

She permitted herself a thin smile — so thin it might have escaped notice.

'Comrade, you are not very politically aware.' She held up her hand. 'No matter. You deserve some instruction on why we do what we do — or don't do.

'Our involvement in sabotage is confined to maximum effect for minimum endeavour. The *Herenwyck* is a good example. The *Frielinghaus* ought to have been.' I hung my head.

'Random sabotage has the opposite effect to that intended. It puts our members to unnecessary risk. It has very little effect on production, and alienates the German working class, on whom we depend for the future. The more the allies carpet-bomb Germany the fiercer will be Germany's will to fight. Hitler is the beneficiary.[1]

[1]Against this, interrogation of German soldiers after capture demonstrated how

'In Yugoslavia and one or two other occupied territories acts of terrorism — killing your Germans — which provoke brutal retaliation may indeed provoke further acts of defiance, and so create a revolutionary situation. This is emphatically not the case in Germany. Our task here is to collect information and relay it to the Soviet Union.

'Espionage, Kersten, is not dramatic. It is having the right person in the right place at the right time. Collecting the information and transmitting instructions to agents is far more important than wrenching a railway line out of place or shooting a German soldier. You have a vital role. Do you understand, Comrade Kersten?'

'Yes, I do,' I replied. I could not bring myself to say 'Comrade', nor 'Frau Jansen'. I was too frightened to point out that she should have used my code name of Karl.

She gazed long and intently at me. 'Very well, you may go.'

I backed out of that room, miserable and downcast.

Two days later we learned that the Gestapo had arrested the Schulze-Boysen group. This Berlin communist cell, headed by a young aristocrat, Harold Schulze-Boysen, an intelligence officer in the Luftwaffe, had no direct links with Die Wasserkante, but there were two contacts common to both groups. One was in Königsberg. His name was Oskar. The other was in Rostock. And that was Magda, who had saved me from the Gestapo. I was ordered to eliminate both of them to break the chain that would lead to Die Wasserkante. It was essential for the Gestapo to confirm their deaths, and Inge would report accordingly. Thus I was trapped.

Back in my room I looked up the train timetable. One left for Königsberg via Hamburg at 7.15 a.m. I lay on the bed and thought about Inge Werner and Oma Jansen. Could Inge's mother (who was illegitimate) be Oma Jansen's daughter, making Inge Oma's granddaughter? The ages fitted. So did the politics. So too did the too-close affection. I was dozing off when there was a soft knock on the door.

I jumped to the floor. The 'knock on the door' spelt Gestapo, only it was too quiet; too conspiratorial. The Gestapo would batter down the woodwork. Cautiously I opened the door. A

---

the morale of German servicemen was eroded by fear for the fate of their families in bombed cities. The unquantifiable aspect of the Allied bomber offensive should not be ignored.

figure stood in the shadows, hat well pulled down. 'For you,' he muttered, handing me a Walther 7.65mm. 'I will call for it when you return.'

So it was to be death by shooting. Hartoch, of course, had taught me how to handle guns. I checked it. The weapon was oiled, and each chamber loaded. Tied to the butt was a cotton bag with some more cartridges.

It was raining heavily when I caught the train for Hamburg. During my sleepless night I had worked out a plan to save Magda.

I left the train at Hamburg and made my way to a cabaret, Zur Kayute, in the district of St Paulis. The madam there (for the cabaret was a brothel) was an occasional agent on whom I'd called a few times to collect data about shipping movements. She was a blonde, brassy, hard-faced bitch of thirty-five or so, but she'd taken a fancy to me: 'the-son-she'd-never-had' sort of thing (and never would). Anyway Maria could, I reckoned, be counted on.

I put my scheme to her and described Magda in detail. Maria took it all in then left. Two hours later she returned with a new identity card. 'From now on your friend will be known as Irmgard Gottlieb and her occupation is barmaid. I will employ her here and she can stay at my place until the coast's clear.'

At the station a train was about to start for Berlin, where I could get a connection to Königsberg.

A Berlin railway station at the height of the war: uniforms everywhere, badges of every kind and description: service badges, wound badges, U-boat badges, insignia for this, insignia for that. And the constant refrain: *'Papiere, bitte'* as German military police, wearing a half-shield round their necks like wine waiters, checked all identities. Total thoroughness. Total war.

This was the high noon of Nazi success, September 1942. Europe from the Atlantic to the Volga, from the Arctic Circle to the Mediterranean, was in Hitler's hands. His troops had stormed into Stalingrad, and in Africa stood a mere sixty miles from Alexandria. His U-boats had almost severed the Atlantic life-line between America and England.

A month earlier, with the capture of the Soviet oil-fields at Maikop in the Caucusus, the official Nazi newspaper, *Völkischer Beobachter*, had trumpeted 'With mathematical certainty we know that the war is won.'

True, in May the RAF had begun an air offensive on German cities with a thousand-bomber raid on Cologne, prompting bitter civilian outrage against the country most Germans wanted as their ally (including, according to *Mein Kampf*, Adolf Hitler!)

The RAF apart, however, the Allies were everywhere on the defensive. In the Far East Germany's ally, Japan, had conquered British, American and Dutch territory ten times greater than the Nippon homeland. Their armies were poised on the threshold of India, with mutinous politicians and mobs there demanding 'Peace with Japan. Quit India.'

The Americans had not even appeared on the European battlefield. The Germans had taken 3,500,000 Russian prisoners, and now controlled a larger proportion of the Soviet population than did Moscow.

The Germans had suffered heavy casualties, but the ranks were filled up with fresh detachments, not least from the European lands friendly to the Reich: Italy, Spain, Hungary, Finland, Rumania, Bulgaria, Flemish Belgium, parts of Holland, Croatia, Slovenia, the Baltic lands, Ukraine, Crimea, the Kuban. The occupied Soviet territories were yielding a huge crop of collaborators; not least the formidable Cossacks. No wonder there was such a babble of foreign tongues; French workers, and Ukrainian volunteers; Norwegian engineers and Spanish soldiers of the Blue Division.

Goebbels's Propaganda Ministry harped on the European crusade against Asiatic Bolshevism. Polyglot Berlin seemed to supply the evidence.

*   *   *

Once aboard the train I went to the toilet and checked my pistol and a flick knife I had bought as a back-up! I did not fancy having to use it. Oskar, the Königsberg sleeper, was a powerfully built keep-fit fanatic. He owned a small boat-building concern. I had called on him once or twice, and had no compunction about killing him. I just didn't want to fight him.

The train rolled into Königsberg and I confirmed times of departure from the station that evening. I reckoned I had 3½ hours to carry out my assignment, and I walked towards the exit with my sailing book in my hand. From experience I knew that the military police simply waves through sailors on leave, and so it transpired.

Königsberg was entirely undamaged. It was outside the range of the RAF, and wore a peace-time air. The Russians had been unable to hit the capital of East Prussia because the Soviet Air Force had been effectively destroyed in the first five days of the German invasion. So, for the first time in many months I walked through untouched, untroubled streets.

Oskar lived in a wooden bungalow in a park beside a lake. He lived alone, his wife having deserted him. His black-out was not perfect (Königsberg was not at all air-raid conscious). I could see a glimmer of light in a side window. I crept closer. The house was isolated, but courting couples might be anywhere behind the bushes. I waited in the shadow of a tree for twenty minutes, then crept nearer still, and paused for another ten minutes.

Now I crept right up to the cabin and peered through a small split in the shutters — no curtains. There he was, this hefty Prussian, fiddling with the knobs of his radio. I could hear music. Satisfied, Oskar sat down at a table and picked up a magazine. I moved towards the outer door, taking out my pistol and releasing the safety catch. Gently I placed my hand on the door handle. To my relief it opened quietly. On my left a strip of lighting shone from the room in which Oskar was sitting. I knew he was facing the door, but wouldn't have time to move.

I took two steps forward and flung the door open. He recognized me. I think a smile was dawning on him as I pumped two bullets into his left side. He slumped across the table. Dead.

Outside all was quiet. I made my way back to the railway station through deserted streets. At the station the loudspeakers were blaring a *Sondermeldung*, a special communiqué: 'The Swastika flag is flying over Stalingrad's city hall. Russia's last lifeline with the oil-rich south is cut.' The announcer's triumphant voice droned on. The message ended with the strains of *Deutschland, Deutschland über alles*, followed by the *Horst Wessel Lied*. Well, it took my mind off the recent bloody business.

Now to Berlin and Rostock and Magda.

Rostock was no Königsberg. You couldn't move a hundred metres without spotting devastation. The bombers had demolished whole rows of houses near the docks. Magda's street had its share of smouldering rubble, but her home — a ground-floor flat in a three-storey house reserved for prostitutes — was still standing, although wooden boards had replaced windows.

I knocked on the timber to the tempo of a waltz repeated three times. Magda opened the door and flung her arms round my neck. Brusquely I removed her. She bolted the door and turned to me.

'What is wrong? Why are you here? I have no information for you. You are not due for a data collection.' Then, in a different, more relaxed tone, 'But I am glad you're here anyway. I've been frightened by the bombing. We've no electricity, only candles.'

I cut into her breathless talk. 'Get your papers.' Magda had been in Die Wasserkante for more than two years. She knew the essence of speed without questions. She fetched her documents. Her registration card listed her as a Public Woman — a whore. Her medical card declared her free from venereal disease. It had a weekly date. She blushed. Magda had not chosen to be a professional. Her boyfriend — a Red — had been taken by the Gestapo. She had been with him at the moment of arrest, and, naked, had been dragged off for interrogation. Her boyfriend disappeared. She was given the choice of a brothel or a concentration camp. She chose the brothel.

I held the papers over the candle until they started to burn.

'For heaven's sake what are you doing?' she exploded. 'I have to go for a check-up tomorrow. If I fail to report the police will come for me. It'll be the camp this time.'

'Listen carefully,' I said. 'You will not report tomorrow night. You will stay with a friend of mine; a woman friend.'

I explained about the arrest in Berlin, and that she was the vital link between Berlin and Bremen. I did not explain that I was supposed to be her executioner.

'Why have they sent you?' she asked.

I showed her her new identity papers.

'They look a damn sight better than the ones I had.'

'Now, Irmgard Gottlieb, are you ready to leave this hole? Ah, and one more thing — have the police checked round here for survivors?'

'Yes. They know I'm alive. Does it matter?'

'Yes, it does. Is there anyone else in the building?'

'No, I'm alone.'

'Mmm. Then hurry up will you? I want to get an early train out of Rostock.'

I looked around the room. There wasn't much left after the bombing. If I set it alight the police would simply assume the candle was the culprit. With the bombing there had been, and would be again, no one would search for the charred remains of a whore.

We were ready to leave. Suddenly the air-raid siren sounded. 'Magda, remember this: if we get separated get on the Hamburg train and go to the Zur Kayute cabaret in St Paulis, ask for Maria — she's the manageress. You're expected as Irmgard Gottlieb, mind. Tell her I sent you. She's completely trustworthy. Meanwhile we'll get going. Then I'll return and set this place ablaze.'

We left separately. After six minutes the bombers arrived. 'Irmgard' kept on walking. I dived for cover. 'Give it ten minutes,' I thought. But the bombs did the job for me. When I returned I saw the whole street was burning furiously, 'Irmgard's house included. Once again pure chance had completed my resistance task.

However, I wasted no more time philosophizing but made my way to the railway station as the sirens wailed the 'All Clear.' 'Irmgard' was safely delivered to Maria. I returned to Bremen. The links had been cut. Inge reported to Oma Jansen that Gestapo reports from Königsberg and Rostock confirmed the murder of Oskar and the presumed death through aerial bombardment of the former Red suspect and Public Woman. Die Wasserkante was safe.

Seven

The Strange Failure in the Caucasus

No one who did not live through it can comprehend the impact that the battle of Stalingrad had on the German people and the occupied territories. Until November 1942 the German Army had always been victorious. Occasional setbacks, true, but the grand pattern was one of stunning victory. 'Invincible' was the title of a Nazi propaganda film. It seemed too near the truth.

Then in the course of a single month the Afrika Korps and Italians were hurled back at El Alamein, American forces landed in North Africa and, most terrible of all, the huge, well-armed Sixth Army was surrounded at Stalingrad.

A horror of Russia's snow wastes gripped the German people. Their husbands, sons, lovers were out there. Defeat at Alamein was almost acceptable. The war in the desert had see-sawed for two years anyway. And even if, this time, the British went all the way it would be a comfortable prison billet for the captives — North Africa was the 'gentlemanly war'. Russia was a barbarous one. There castration was the frequent lot of prisoners taken after a particularly bloody battle. And now a quarter of a million German soldiers were encircled 2,000 kilometres from home.

To mention Napoleon was considered defeatist, yet the spectre of the French Army's fate haunted millions of German families.

Hitler had deliberately tempted fate by invading Russia on the very day — 22 June — which Napoleon had chosen in 1812. When the German Army successfully repelled the Soviet winter offensive in 1941-2 Hitler boasted that he had conquered the elements which had 'beaten another man 130 years ago'. Hitler's iron will triumphed over the doubts and anxieties of his generals in that first winter campaign.

The Führer insisted on holding on to towns which the advancing Red Army had by-passed. They were named 'hedgehogs' and supplied from the air. Those generals who said it couldn't be done were confounded. Several, including Field Marshal von Brauchitsch, nominal Commander-in-Chief of the Army, resigned or were dismissed. One, Colonel-General Graf von Sponeck, was sentenced to death for permitting the Russians to establish a bridgehead on the Crimea at Kerch.[1] (Hitler was obsessively concerned with holding the Crimea, 'the aircraft carrier of the Black Sea.')

By March 1942 the Soviet attacks had petered out. The German Army, which could have been overwhelmed had it retreated, was able to launch a series of devastating counter-blows from the hedgehogs Hitler had insisted on holding. Within four months the situation had been transformed, with Soviet armies being encircled and annihilated from Leningrad to Rostov.

An exultant Führer — who, not content with being supreme head of the Wehrmacht, had taken over from Brauchitsch as C-in-C of the Army — contemptuously dismissed the German officer corps as a bunch of old women. *They* had been prepared to flee. *He* had stood like a rock.

From the summer of 1942 a gap opened between the Generals and the Führer to whom they had pledged their oath of allegiance 'unto death'.

In July 1942 Russia faced the greatest crisis of the war. Bursting into the Northern Caucusus, across the river Don and piercing the Soviet flank from across the Kerch Isthmus, the panzer divisions of General von Kleist rolled across the flat Kuban countryside at the alarming, almost unbelievable, rate of 100 kilometres a day. Stalin issued a desperate Order of the Day commanding his troops to 'stand or die'. The Soviet soldiers were doing neither. They were deserting to the Germans in such numbers that by 1943 *every seventh soldier in the German Army* was a former Soviet serviceman.[2] The soldiers crossing over to the German lines were mainly Turkomen, Cossacks, Georgians: minorities who had suffered Moscow's vicious persecution.

The Soviet positions in the Caucusus were vanishing as swiftly as snow in the sun. Without the oil of the Caucusus Russia could

[1]Sponeck's sentence was commuted to life imprisonment. However, he was executed later in the war, *pour encourager les autres*.

[2]See *Against Two Evils*, by Hans von Herwarth.

not hope to win the war. With its oil Hitler was convinced he could not lose it. The conquest of the Caucusus was Hitler's principal economic aim in invading Russia. Yet quite suddenly the advance petered out. In mid-August the Germans were racing for the oil-fields of Grozny. Three months later they still had not reached them, and they never did. For defeat at Stalingrad — hundreds of kilometres to the north — forced the Germans to execute a swift and final retreat.

But why did the Caucusus offensive fail? Hitler blamed the initial Commander of the Army Group, Field Marshal Wilhelm List, and removed him, giving command to the panzer general Erwin von Kleist. But two of Kleist's senior officers were communists — Lt-General Vincenz Müller,[1] Chief of Staff to the spearhead Seventeenth Army of Colonel-General Ruoff, and General Oskar Ritter von Niedermayer, commanding a division of Turkomen volunteers. The Soviet spy ring in Switzerland referred in messages to Moscow to the Bavarian generals who were Soviet sympathizers. Both Niedermayer and Müller were Bavarians. How many more in this Army Group were secretly on Stalin's side and influential enough to sabotage an offensive which seemed to have every prospect of success? Why did Hitler transfer troops from the Caucasian front to Stalingrad, a move which would — and did — engulf an army in futile, costly street fighting? His obsession with 'taking Stalin's town' is always given as the reason. Perhaps he also received deliberately flawed advice.[2] With disaster at Stalingrad, the Führer's famed intuition received a mortal blow.

Resistance in all its forms, gained heart from the growing likelihood of Germany's defeat.

*   *   *

The chill sense of foreboding among growing numbers of Germans communicated itself to people in the occupied countries. I sensed it in my travels 'on leave', so to speak, to my

[1]After the war Müller built up the East German Army.

[2]'It is not speed that matters now; you had better slow down.' Message to General von Schweppenburg, commanding the 40th Panzer Corps, from Army HQ General Staff (quoted by Schweppenburg in *Irish Defence Review*, 1950).
Britain and America were so sure the Russians would lose the Caucusus that they prepared an Anglo-US intervention called Operation Velvet. Moscow indignantly rejected the scheme 'as unacceptable interference'. (Marshal Andrei Grechko's *Battle for the Caucusus*.)

homeland.

Once it had seemed as natural to go to work in Germany as to seek a new life in America. I had been looked up to as a rather smart lad; 'hearing the grass grow' was the expression. But no longer.

Now my one-time friends and acquaintances looked at me askance. Now I was a collaborator. Again and again I was approached by old school mates demanding to know what I was doing working for the Nazis. I should come home and join them in the struggle.

To listen to them you would think Holland was aflame; everyone — it seemed — was in the Resistance, sabotaging the Wehrmacht, harbouring Jews. I found it hard to understand how there remained a single German alive in Holland, except that I knew from Hartoch that resistance was ineffective and that what there was of the Dutch underground had been so effectively penetrated by the Germans that British agents were arrested as soon as they parachuted to earth. In some cases the Germans already had the agents' names and numbers.

Eight

Pattern of a Putsch

In the spring of 1943 resistance to Hitler crystallized in the German Army. Defeat was the spur. At Stalingrad 90,000 Germans had surrendered — and another 150,000 had died. In Tunisia 160,000 Germans and Italians faced certain capture. With the United States building up its forces in Britain, with increasing day and night air assaults by the USAF and the RAF on German cities, the imminent invasion of Italy and clear evidence that the Soviet Army was gathering together its strength for a summer offensive, there was no possibility of total German victory. In the eyes of a number of German generals the best that could be hoped for was to negotiate peace in the West — evacuating France, the Low Countries, Scandinavia — while continuing to resist the Soviets.

This, of course, was anathema to the pro-Russian elements, who were genuinely afraid that, despite the Western Allies' demand for 'unconditional surrender', the West could be tempted to conclude a separate peace. The two most influential officers representing the view were the recently promoted Major-General Ritter von Niedermayer and Colonel Klaus von Stauffenberg: the former because he was a dedicated communist working to save Russia (and a Germany that would be allied to Russia), the latter because he believed in a compact with the East and had vague socialist aspirations which he thought could best be realized through a deal with Moscow.

The 'Easterners' accepted that they had not the slightest prospect of winning over German generals to a policy of peace in the East while continuing the war in the West. Their only practical course was to urge peace on both fronts.

Those German generals captured at Stalingrad — notably von

Seydlitz, and later Field Marshal Paulus — had formed themselves into a Free German Committee, broadcasting from Moscow assurances that the greatness and glory of the German General Staff would be recognized by victorious Russia. There were enough German generals persuaded by this propaganda (for hadn't Soviet Russia offered training facilities to the Reichswehr in the twenties?) at least to consider the possibility of a truce in the East and West.

All this naturally assumed that the Führer and the Nazi last-ditchers would be removed or liquidated.

Adolf Hitler had made clear his unalterable resolve to continue the struggle 'until five past twelve'. There would be no eleventh-hour surrender; no repetition of 1918.

Moreover, there was not the faintest prospect of the Allies making peace with the Nazi regime. If the British had refused Hitler's overtures, his 'appeal to reason' in the desperate days of 1940, why should the Big Three, now advancing on all fronts, agree to stop short of Berlin?

Whatever the outcome, even the most politically obtuse German officer — and there was no lack of such individuals — could see that the removal of Hitler (and probably Goering, Goebbels and Himmler as well) was the essential precondition of any move towards an armistice.

Already in March 1943 such an attempt had been mounted.

Hitler had announced his intention of visiting Central Army headquarters at Smolensk. Several times previously preparations had been made to assassinate him: each abandoned because he changed his plans at the last moment. That was the Führer's pattern: part precaution, part sheer vagary.

Two officers — Henning von Tresckow and Fabian von Schlabrendorff — assembled a plastic bomb which would be detonated when acid burned through wire which held the detonator on 'safety'. Its shape bore a close resemblance to a couple of brandy bottles. Carefully parcelled in brown paper, this deadly cargo was to be placed on Hitler's aircraft, timed to explode when the plane was over Minsk on its return journey to the Führer's headquarters in Rastenburg.

This time everything went as planned. As Hitler's flight was about to depart from Smolensk a staff car drew up and Schlabrendorff emerged holding his carefully packed, paper-covered 'brandy bottles' duly primed.

'Could you possibly deliver these bottles as a gift to General Tresckow's friend, General Helmut Stieff, at Rastenburg?' he asked one of Hitler's aides, Colonel Brandt. 'Do be careful of them — it's really fine stuff.' Brandt readily accepted the package and stored it in the luggage hold.

The Führer's flight took off with a large fighter escort, and Tresckow and Schlabrendorff's car, with Field Marshal von Kluge in close attendance, raced back to Smolensk to await the news. The conspirators estimated that the bomb would explode in thirty minutes from take-off. Half an hour passed; an hour; two hours. Then the routine call from Rastenburg to say that the Führer's flight had landed safely.

With astounding nonchalance Schlabrendorff at once set off to get hold of the faulty bomb. He arrived at Rastenburg on 14 March, bringing with him a package containing two genuine bottles of brandy which he handed to Colonel Brandt. Von Tresckow had already telephoned Brandt telling him there had been a mistake — the brandy was not the right quality — and would he please hand back the package in exchange for the correct one. Brandt did so, and a relieved Schlabrendorff dismantled the bomb in the privacy of a railway sleeping compartment on the way to Berlin, where he reported to fellow-conspirators on the staff of the Home Army on the failure of 'Operation Flash'.[1]

The Smolensk venture had embraced such leading figures as Admiral Canaris, chief of the Abwehr or German Military Intelligence, who had surrounded himself with anti-Nazi aristocrats. On the fringe, and somewhat equivocal in his attitude, was the commander of the Army Group centre, Field Marshal von Kluge: an ambitious, able officer who would go along with the conspirators if they were successful but would take no initiative himself, or be caught with the consequences of failure. He was, however, compromised by evidence — which had fallen into the hands of his chief staff officer, General Tresckow — that he had accepted from Hitler a large financial gift and a building licence as a gift on his sixtieth birthday.

By such sweeteners Hitler reckoned to keep him loyal, but the taint of corruption was not likely to enhance Kluge's reputation among his fellow-officers. So Tresckow used the information if not to blackmail Kluge, at least to keep him in line.

[1]The account of this episode is based on Schlabrendorff's *Offizieren gegen Hitler* and von Tresckow's observations heard by Jakob Kersten.

Tresckow was at this point one of the key conspirators. From the start of the invasion of Russia he had collected round him at Army Group Centre a bevy of anti-Hitler plotters. He claimed credit for nullifying Hitler's notorious Commissar Order, by which every Soviet political instructor was to be summarily executed on capture.

Tresckow had been closely involved with an earlier attempt to grab Hitler and hold him hostage while elderly anti-Nazi generals — notably Colonel-General Ludwig Beck — cobbled together a new government. This unlikely plot was concocted at Borisov, which was Central Army Group HQ in the early days of the Russian war, while the Panzer divisions were striking triumphantly forward and practically every German general was dreaming of glory and promotion, not treason. Even Tresckow's own chief, Field Marshal von Bock, had no intention of assisting or condoning such hare-brained schemes. He was too intent on getting to Moscow.

Yet it is significant that though he must have been aware of Tresckow's sentiments von Bock did not turn in his chief staff officer. The corps loyalty of the German Army took precedence over everything else.

As Hitler's legions began the long trip home in the winter of 1942-43 — what Churchill so aptly called 'the hinge of fate' — some of those aristocratic militarists who had been merely contemptuous of the Nazis turned to outright opposition.

True, some of them were rendered fairly harmless. A number were retired. One, Field Marshal von Witzleben, secretly an out-and-out foe of Hitler who was scheduled to take command in the West, went down with a severe attack of piles,[1] and his post was given to Field Marshal von Rundstedt, who was too downy a bird to be caught in any conspiracy.

Even so, by spring 1943 the military plotters sworn to take Hitler's life were strongly established in the following:

Army Group centre on the Eastern Front
The Home, or Reserve, Army in Berlin
German Military Command (von Stuelpnagel) in Paris
German Military Command (von Falkenhausen) in Brussels
The Abwehr Military Intelligence (Admiral Canaris).

Two more plans to eliminate the Führer had to be abandoned

[1] Piles have a lot to answer for. Napoleon suffered from them at Waterloo.

shortly after the Smolensk failure, and the anti-Nazi generals, with their civilian collaborators headed by Carl Goerdeler, former Mayor of Leipzig, resolved to try to broaden the resistance front, and the potential alternative Government, by forming a pact with the Left, including the communists.

At this juncture of the war the military and Hitler stood in equilibrium; uncomfortable to be sure, but still roughly in balance.

The defeat at Stalingrad had robbed the Führer of any title to infallibility. It had also torn to shreds what remained of Reichsmarschall Goering's reputation after his abortive boast 'No bombs will fall on Berlin'. (The first bombs had fallen in August 1940!) He had assured the Wehrmacht he could keep the Sixth Army at Stalingrad supplied from the air. He failed to keep his promise. So the Luftwaffe — perhaps the most Nazi of the three Services — had stumbled fatefully. Hitler had got rid of some of the weaker vessels at the top of the military hierarchy: Brauschitsch, as already mentioned, from the C-in-C post; Franz Halder, Chief of the Army General Staff; Ritter von Leeb, who had commanded the stalled drive on Leningrad; Colonel-General Hoepner for retreating before Moscow (Hoepner became a leading plotter). He advanced a number of supposedly tougher generals, but, by and large, he had to admit that he could not do without the military. He relied on the loyal if self-interested support of the Army, so that professional German officers recovered some of the standing they surrendered when they had cravenly counselled retreat in Russia in the previous winter. Then Hitler had proved them wrong. Now, however, at Stalingrad and in North Africa, events had proved *him* wrong. If the enemy was to be kept at bay long enough for the miracle weapons — the V1 flying bomb and the V2 rocket — to come into play, the Army's prestige had to be maintained. Senior officers were therefore permitted a large degree of freedom from party surveillance; the Army was permitted to regulate its own.

Thus treason flourished despite the mordant scepticism of people like Field Marshal von Rundstedt and the 'hear-no-evil, see-no-evil' attitude of non-political generals such as Field Marshal von Manstein — the brilliant 'escape artist' who had rescued the southern German Army Group from encirclement and annihilation.

Consequently it was fairly simple to arrange rendezvous with other elements of the Resistance movement.

*   *   *

My intimation that such a meeting had been arranged came from Hans in April 1943. 'We are going to Berlin in five days. The generals have sought us out.'

'Where do I fit in?' I asked.

'You will act as a courier. So you will have to know these people. Naturally, you will take no part in the discussion. You are just part of the wallpaper. But it will be instructive. Perhaps historic. Although, to be honest, I am not optimistic about the outcome.'

Berlin presented a spectacle of mounting devastation. As we walked from General von Niedermayer's house on the Hagenstrasse, where we had spent the night, to the meeting-place at 1a Davoserstrasse, about a half-hour journey, I could see the evidence everywhere. When I was last in the capital bomb-damaged houses were propped up with wooden supports until repair men could get to work. Now bombed buildings were left untouched; only the rubble from the streets was removed to permit the free flow of traffic.

Davoserstrasse, however, was unscathed. By bombs, that is. It must have been given 24-hours-a-day maintenance, so immaculate was its appearance.

Hans rang the bell. A woman opened the door. Hans said, 'I have come to see a Herr Deutsch.'

She smiled. 'That's me. You have come to the right address.'

Present in the upstairs drawing-room and sitting round a large table were von Niedermayer, who introduced us: Generals von Hase and Fellgiebel, Henning von Tresckow and Colonel-General Jänecke, Major Schwerin from the Luftwaffe, Colonel von Hofacker and a civilian, Haushofer[1].

The officers in their uniforms made us civilians feel dowdy. Civilians in wartime Germany were meant to accept second-class citizenship, which is why everyone did the utmost to get into

[1]General Paul von Hase, City Commandant of Berlin; Major Karl von Schwerin, ADC to Hase; Colonel Caesar von Hofacker, Luftwaffe Staff Officer at General von Stuelpnagel's Headquarters, Army of Occupation Paris — former industrialist; General Erich Fellgiebel, Chief of Signals, Armed Services HQ; Henning von Tresckow, Chief of Staff to the central German Army group in the East; Ernst Jänecke, commanded German troops in the Crimea; George Albrecht Haushofer, son of the noted professor of geopolitics who exercised much influence on Adolf Hitler's theory of *Lebensraum*, a living space for Germany.

some sort of uniform — even if it were only a postman's or a railway guard's.

Hans had told me to utter not a word, so I sat with my back to the wall, well away from the table, and kept still as a graven image. Naturally, I made no notes of the discussion. But every detail was etched on my mind.

Colonel Caesar von Hofacker spoke for the peace-in-the-West faction, then Hans broke in. Where Niedermayer was the quiet, persuasive purveyor of the classical Bismarck policy towards Russia, Hans burst forth with the passionate plea of the convinced communist. He accused von Hofacker of representing only a small circle of industrialists while the German workers yearned for socialism and an economic union with the Soviets. Hofacker turned white and clenched his fists. He rejected the idea as ludicrous.

Niedermayer then chipped in with an argument designed to appeal to the generals who recalled the happy days when the Reichswehr trained in Russia with the benign blessing of a communist government. As one who had been present — who indeed had negotiated that special relationship — Niedermayer was listened to with total silence and deep respect. No one suspected for one moment that he was a Party member, an executive of the militant Left underground. He argued persuasively that Russia was the only one of the Big Three ranged against the Reich who would allow a Hitler-free Germany freedom of action.

Niedermayer's words made a profound impact. Even Hofacker appeared impressed — he was probably calculating the impact on his own industrial holdings. Then Henning von Tresckow, the man from the East, leant forward. He had actually prepared an attempt on Hitler's life. He had risked his own. He had automatic call on the admiration and loyalty of his fellow-officers.

'My dear Niedermayer,' he said. 'Your experience of Russia is ten years out of date. We can expect no mercy from Moscow. We have no choice but to make peace with the West. With the East we have no choice but to wage unrelenting war.'

I looked at this personification of German militarism, proud bearer of the Knight's Cross of the Iron Cross, who had gone along with Hitler's conquests[1] and now wanted to spare Ger-

---

[1] He was, however, one of the earliest to turn against the Führer's bloody excesses.

many the horrors that Germany had visited on Eastern Europe and Russia. This man was as much a foe of Die Wasserkante as the Nazis. How could we co-operate with him? I looked over to Niedermayer.

He was sitting with lowered head. He knew (as Tresckow and the others did not) that within a month the Free German Officers' Committee in Moscow — soldiers taken prisoner at Stalingrad — would be issuing an appeal similar to the one he had made to the meeting. He sensed then that there was nothing fruitful to be gained from collaboration with the generals.

The union of German Officers duly issued its proclamation from Moscow.

It was a cleverly worded proclamation designed to appeal to patriotic Germans concerned about their country's plight. 'We speak', declared the Union, 'in the first place to the Army chiefs . . . do what is necessary or it will be done without you or even against you. Declare war on the disastrous Nazi regime . . . remove the Führer from command [note: not kill him]. Take the initiative now.'

About the same period the first serious public rift opened up between the Soviets and their Western partners. Berlin announced that the bodies of 14,000 Polish officers had been discovered in the forest of Katyn, near Smolensk, in German-occupied Russia. Independent forensic evidence — provided by the Swiss Red Cross — clearly indicated they had been murdered in 1940 when Soviet troops had been in control of eastern Poland. In short, the Russians had murdered the Poles: who were now Stalin's ally.

The British and American Governments denounced publicly the whole business as a Nazi propaganda trick; privately, and to each other, they expressed deep unease. Polish forces were fighting most valorously in North Africa, and were assigned to invade Italy. Other Poles were gathering in the Middle East to reinforce their comrades. An open breach between Moscow and the exiled Polish Government in London could do untold harm to the morale of the Polish forces and damage the unity of the Big Three.

Dr Goebbels brilliantly exploited the Western Allies' embarrassment and convinced many in Germany that the unnatural alliance of capitalism and communism, always fragile, was on the point of disintegrating.

At a stroke the likelihood of the German resistance forming a united front from nationalists to communists diminished to vanishing point. The Westerners exultantly pointed to the breach as evidence that they could deal with London and Washington at the expense of Moscow. The 'Easterners' had no convincing answer.

The seeds of the plot to overthrow Hitler and the role of Torgau in that conspiracy were planted at this juncture. So too was the decision of Niedermayer and Die Wasserkante to have nothing to do with the 'Western' generals and their scheme to substitute themselves for the Führer.

Nine

Torgau

On the morning of 30 July 1943 I set sail on the steamship *Emily Sauber* as assistant engineer bound for Gothenburg in neutral Sweden. Oma Jansen, Hans concurring, had ordered me to contact our Stockholm representative and to begin my political education in preparation for a return to a new socialized Germany after hostilities. For me, it seemed the war was over.

We were a day out when the ship's Merchant Marine flag was lowered and the naval war flag raised. Overnight the Merchant Navy was brought under the war laws of the Armed Forces. I had become an auxiliary officer in the Nazi Kriegsmarine.

Therefore when the ship docked at Gothenburg and an armed guard was placed at the gangway to prevent crew members from going ashore in a neutral country I had no alternative to breaking out. I had to rendezvous with my contact at nine that evening.

I tried to bluff my way past — 'Just an hour with a woman.' The guard raised his rifle menacingly so I kicked him on the shin, and simultaneously pinioned his hand to the rail with my knife. He screamed in anguish as I made off — down the gangplank, along the quayside, boots thudding on the asphalt, head down — and then I was staring at two fawn raincoats belonging to the Swedish Police force. 'Your papers?' That was merely a formality. Within hours I was on a German ship charged with desertion and sabotage: desertion because I had left my ship against orders; sabotage because in wounding a crew member attached to the Armed Forces I had 'damaged the German nation's ability to wage war'. Had I knifed a mere civilian that would have constituted a much lesser crime. I comforted myself that at least I was not suspected of underground activity. At most, I thought, I faced two or three years in gaol. Unpleasant, but reasonably safe.

If only I had known! We arrived at Wilhelmshaven, and I was transferred to a military barracks 80 kilometres away. There I was informed that I would stand trial before Staatsrichter (judge) Tiedeman of the Second Admiralty Division of the North Sea Command.

The *Obermaat* (staff-sergeant), a downy old veteran of the Kaiser's day, gave me a kind of consumer's guide to military prisons. Tonelessly he reeled them off: 'Langres, not such a bad place. Then there is Halle: they specialize in decapitation there. And there is Torgau. That place is something. You'd be better off dead than in Torgau. From Torgau you go to the *Feldgefangenerab-teilung* (field prison unit) of the *Bewährungbataillon* (penal battalion). You do not get out of there until you are dead on the battlefield.'

'You are Dutch, aren't you?' he added.

'Yes.'

'We had a Dutch fellow a while back. He was three days late returning to duty with his unit — volunteer for the Waffen SS — got twenty years hard labour.'

Next day I was taken handcuffed to the court room and told that, according to the rules, I would be prosecuted and defended by the same counsel.

The room was long, drab and musty. In front of me was a table with three chairs on the far side, and behind them three flags: the red, white and black swastika banner of the Party and State and two naval flags emblazoned with the swastika and the traditional German Maltese cross. Above the banners was a large portrait of Adolf Hitler. On each side of me stood two motionless military policemen: on my left, at a small table, sat the prosecutor — who switched to my right when acting as my defender.

The judge, an Army officer, took his seat, flanked by two Naval officers. The prosecutor established that I was a Dutch-born assistant engineer serving on the *SS Emily Sauber* and that I had come under the German Navy Code of Conduct during the voyage to Gothenburg.

Judge Tiedeman looked down on me: 'Kersten, do you understand the implications of this?'

'Yes, sir,' I replied, inwardly quaking at the possibilities.

The sailor I had wounded — a Sudetenlander, and naturally fanatically Nazi — gave evidence as to my assault on him. There were also sworn statements from the captain of the *Emily Sauber* and the Secretary to the German Consul in Gothenburg.

Then the prosecutor crossed the floor and argued in mitigation that I was young, a foreign worker with little knowledge of German laws, and none at all of German naval conduct.

In his summing up he asked for leniency in one breath and the death sentence in the next.

Judge Tiedeman brought matters to a conclusion. 'You must appreciate, Kersten, that your position is analogous to that of a lieutenant in the Navy. You abused that position to try to gain entry to a foreign country. You deliberately deserted ship when it was understaffed. You wilfully caused bodily harm to a German crew member while in the course of his duty to the Fatherland. Such an act of sabotage is inexcusable.'

All this time he had been reading from notes, never once looking at me. Now he raised his head and stared straight at me.

'So far as I am concerned you deserve the death sentence.' His clear, stern voice tolled my fate. I was helped back into my seat, shaking, dazed, sweating.

The court-martial members retired. Minutes later they returned. Again I rose to my feet. Shuffling documents . . . whispers . . . covert glances. Then the President, the cold judge, pronounced my doom. The death sentence on both counts. I particularly noted these words 'on both counts'. Would they hang me twice? But the President was still speaking.

'This sentence is mandatory under German law. However, on account of your youth and the fact that you have served Germany faithfully for three years, and because you are of pure Aryan blood, a special plea for clemency will be lodged on your behalf with the District Commanding Officer, who must confirm the sentence. The plea will be unanimously endorsed by this court. We shall recommend mercy. The prisoner will remain closely confined awaiting the outcome. Have you anything to say?'

'No, sir.'

Suddenly all those in the court were on their feet. Shoulders back, heads held high and every eye fixed on the portrait of the Führer as they intoned 'Heil Hitler'. The proceedings were ended.

I was removed to a near-by cell-block and ushered into a routine box: small window, iron bars, bucket and bunk. I started to wonder about death. Those Germans I'd seen lying on the streets after raids seemed perfectly tranquil. Whenever I saw a corpse with a smile I assumed death had been a blessing. I was trying to condition my mind to accept it.

One day, maybe two weeks after my trial, the door opened and an Army lieutenant stood in the door. 'Are you the Dutchman?'

I nodded. He threw a packet of cigarettes on my bunk. Before I could utter a word he was gone. I removed each cigarette singly. There was a note. All it said was: 'Courage. We will care for you.' The handwriting was Inge's.

Two days later I was summoned to appear before the Court once more.

I stood at attention as a naval officer informed me that the plea for clemency had been successful. My sentence was commuted to fifteen years' imprisonment. Place of detention — Festung Zinna in Torgau.

As I was being sent to a military prison, I had to be clad in German Army uniform; moreover, my civilian clothes would be sent to my home in Zutphen. (They were! The Germans were sticklers for protocol.) I was supplied with a complete field-grey outfit plus cap; one pair of shoes; two garters; two sets of underwear; two pairs of socks; two blankets; one towel; one piece of soap and a rucksack. The swastika-bearing eagle was missing from the tunic and cap to denote that I had been dishonoured. Nor had I epaulettes to denote rank.

Duly handcuffed and escorted by two armed Marines, we set off on the train journey to Torgau, 100 km south of Berlin. The journey was a nightmare interspersed with beauty. In the autumn sunshine the German countryside bore a peaceful, well-ordered serenity. Here and there one could see Polish farmworkers, bearing a broad 'P' on their backs, toiling, apparently contentedly, in the fields. The journey was agonizingly slow, for air-raids had wreaked appalling havoc. Oldenburg . . . Hannover . . . Braunschweig . . . Magdeburg. Everywhere devastation. Our train pulled into Magdeburg at the precise moment the air-raid siren wailed. The town had endured an assault the previous night and we looked out on row after row of flattened houses, only the chimneys standing erect, like deformed, defoliated trees; the air filled with the now unmistakable stench of burning flesh, roasting gently beneath the scorched rubble. The smoke rising from the ruins provided a protective cover against the outside world.

One of my Marine guards whispered, 'Oh, my God, not that.' He was a Magdeburg man with three children. Slowly he rose: 'Just going for a pee, Rudolf.' His senior nodded. The guard picked up his travel bag and disappeared. We never saw him again.

When we arrived in Stettin, Marine Sergeant Rudolf reported his desertion. We got another guard and set off for Berlin. There we had to change trains. I stood on the platform manacled. Passers-by, faces drawn and strained, glanced at my irons and swiftly turned away.

On the first stage my leg was chained to the bench — presumably to prevent any repetition of the guard's vanishing act.

Late afternoon in a misty rain, we got our first sight of Torgau's Festung Zinna. There it stood on top of a hill cleverly planted with spruce to blend into the surrounding countryside, but with the trees planted far enough apart to give no cover to would-be escapers. Guards on duty were accompanied by fierce Alsatian dogs. My guards halted me at the narrow road leading to the main gate. Now, as the mist swirled away, we could see the prison in its forbidding grandeur: a dark granite pile that had seen generations of German soldiers march obediently to oblivion, having slipped from the stern path of service to Kaiser or Führer. My own sense of identity seemed to slide from me as I was transferred into the keeping of a Wehrmacht sergeant.

After four days my handcuffs were removed. Casually the sergeant remarked, 'Dutchman, I can see with half an eye you're no soldier.'

In all innocence I replied, 'Yes, that's right, Sergeant.'

God in heaven, I had with those four words broken three cardinal rules for prisoners of the Wehrmacht!

(i) Never answer without being ordered to do so.

(ii) When ordered, face the gaoler and stand to attention.

(iii) Always address the questioner as 'Herr' — Herr Sergeant, for instance.

Having reminded me of these golden statutes in a raging roar, the sergeant went on with what was clearly his routine welcoming speech.

'At Torgau we make men out of streaks of misery like you. If we fail we bury you. If you become a man you are sent to the BB500.[1]

[1]Penal service battalions; also known from their death-rate as Himmelfahrt Commandos — heaven-bound units, as were the Special Field Battalions.

That is the only way to get out of Torgau. Tomorrow I will report you to the commandant, for unmilitary behaviour. Stand to attention!'

'Let me tell you about the BB500s. They go to the Eastern Front and fling themselves at Bolshevik tanks. Sometimes they get Ivan by lobbing a grenade inside the turret; more often Ivan gets them. Anyway, sooner or later, they go to glory. Now, the Special Field Battalions are a bit less glorious. They clear mines and unexploded bombs. Most of them go with the bombs. If you join a Sonder you don't even have an address for your loved ones to write to to get your remains. Just a simple Fieldpost No. 14169. When they hear that, they know you're a goner. Understand, Dutchman?'

This brave fellow who talked so convincingly of the Eastern Front had, I noticed, no ribbons on his tunic. He had probably, like most of the guards, never been farther east than Torgau, which made them all the more ferocious in their attitude to the prisoners. For if ever they relaxed or showed leniency they might themselves be punished by immediate posting to the Russian front.

My punishment was simpler: two weeks' solitary confinement conferred on me by the Hauptmann's deputy.

The punishment block was on the second floor of the east wing: Feldwebel[1] Günther, NCO in charge.

Günther was a sadist. The only thing that prevented him from venting his hatred physically was the strict Prussian code of military conduct. If he had struck one of us he would have been court-martialled and sent to the fighting front. But short of that, Feldwebel Günther's main preoccupation was to make our life as near to hell as he could get.

'Strip,' he ordered. Every item of clothing was scrutinized. Every part of my body from teeth to scrotum was checked. 'Just one word from you, Dutchman, and you will fall down those steps. Now stand there. At attention.'

So I stood. For three hours. Directly below my line of vision, prisoners would gather at half-hourly intervals. There would be about twenty at a time. They lined themselves up without being ordered to do so, and waited docilely while guards clamped fetters on their legs. They were on their way to the exercise yard.

[1]Feldwebel — sergeant.

As they started forward the iron fetters on the concrete corridor floor sounded like bells, tolling, tolling. The pitiful obedience of concentration-camp victims was if anything exceeded by these German prisoners — many of them once-brave soldiers — so accustomed were they to bow to authority.

Günther caught me watching the scene (though still, of course, at attention). He grinned.

'See the ones with the fetters, Dutchman? They are condemned to die. Tomorrow, the next day, next week. Insubordination, cowardice, failure to obey orders . . . lots of reasons. Some of them are officers; *were* officers. Prison scum have no rank or honour here. One or two might go to Halle for decapitation,' he mused. 'That will be for treason. Do you know they have to lie with their faces upward to the axe? Nice touch, that.

'See over there.' He pointed across to the west wing, where prisoners — neither manacled nor fettered — were being assembled. 'They're for a BB battalion. This time next week, they'll be mixing it with Ivan.'

Finally I was told to dress and was marched off to solitary confinement. Günther ran his hands through his thick blond hair: 'We'll be seeing you again, Dutchman.'

Strangely, the punishment cell was quite spacious. It was, to begin with, a relief to be alone. I spent hours leaning against the cell door, my ear pressed against the steel, just as my old tutor Hartoch had advised me to do in such circumstances. The result was remarkable. After a while I was able to analyse the noises I heard: the names of the guards; their conversation; something of what was happening in other parts of the fortress. It was almost like listening to the radio.

The exchange of news started about eight o'clock in the evening.

'Are you on tomorrow?'

'Yes, I am on.'

'How many this time?' Then the same voice again.

'Oh, just two.'

'Three more and I will have shot another month's home leave.'

They were talking of executions. When they'd reached a quota they got leave.

Sometimes I would be awakened in the early hours with the screams of a prisoner throwing his chained body against the cell door. There would be a whimpering cry of 'mother . . . mother!'

Presumably he was due for execution.

At five in the morning the east wing would come to life. Gates opening . . . closing. Footsteps. Sharp *click-clack* of steel-studded boots . . . the squeak of keys unlocking a cell door; a soft-spoken command, 'Come, prisoner, it is time.' Then the scraping of the fetters. Occasionally a screamed curse. This from outside, in the *Festung* yard.

'*Still gestanden.*' The smack of heels coming together. '*Vorwärts Marsch*' and the even tread of soldiers marching in step. A further clicking (the bolts of rifles?). Yes. And a muffled volley.

Torgau's west wing held short-stay prisoners assigned to drafts of penal or punishment battalions. The north wing was reserved for those awaiting confirmation of sentence. Quite a few belonged to auxiliary units: Croats, Bosnians, Talmucks who had volunteered for service in the Wehrmacht and broken German military law.

On my way back to the punishment block I saw forty prisoners being drilled in the yard. They wore plain German uniforms, but the commands were in a foreign tongue. 'Vlassov Russians, Dutchman,' murmured my guard.

$$* \qquad * \qquad *$$

General Andrei Vlassov had been one of Stalin's favourite, and most successful, young commanders, till, abandoned in a hopeless action, he surrendered and offered to lead a Russian Army of Liberation alongside the Germans.

There was no unified policy towards occupied Russia. But if there had been, if the Nazis had consciously set out to win the hearts and minds of the people in the East, they could have won.

Oskar von Niedermayer, Bavarian Junker, hereditary knight, calmly and persuasively argued actions which he knew would do most damage to the German cause and further the cause of the Soviet Union to which he had pledged allegiance. He advocated the complete break-up of Russia into nationalities — which could not but enrage patriotic Russians — as against the encouragement of dissident rebels, like Vlassov and his men.

A year after Vlassov's conversion to the German cause his 'Army' amounted to a few thousand auxiliaries — some of whom were, in the autumn of 1943, being disciplined at Torgau — and did not amount to corps strength (50,000) until 1944 when it went into action as a separate organization — far too late to influence the result of the war in the East. Andrei Vlassov himself was handed over to Stalin at the end of hostilities and hanged in January 1946. Torgau exemplified the deadly marriage between National Socialism and the Prussian military code. Both were intensely 'physical', rejecting intellectualism, and both appealed enormously to the instincts of the highly disciplined German people. The passion for order found its highest expression in the military code, and National Socialism released the energies and talent of the 'lower orders' who would in the past have been simple recipients of commands. It was as though the French Revolution had been combined with the discipline of the Roman legions. You had no right to retain your personality. At times you almost wanted to become just a number.

* * *

Hauptmann Friedrich was responsible for the harsh, unbending regime of Torgau. I first met him under the following circumstances: suddenly my door was flung open. He stood there immaculate in Wermacht grey, but huge, gross — he must have weighed eighteen stone. Obesity had cost him a fighting job, and resentment burned deep. He stared at me sitting on my bunk, then his pale blue eyes blazed. 'Prisoner,' he squealed (as with many fat men, he had a high-pitched voice), 'when I come into this cell you get to your feet. You should stand to attention against the wall, then you report your full name, why you are here and for how long. Is that clear?'

Without demur I rose to attention and rattled out, 'Prisoner Jakob Kersten, sir, saboteur and deserter. Fifteen years' imprisonment, sir.'

'So' — the Hauptmann's high voice rose a note higher — 'are you deliberately refraining from giving me my title and name?'

'No, sir. I don't know your name,' I replied.

He flushed with rage. 'Prisoner, do you really expect me to believe that after fourteen days you don't know my name? Over the next two weeks you will receive military training with a penal battalion. You will receive half-rations. See to it, Feldwebel.'

The sergeant was standing stiff as a ramrod. *'Jawohl*, Hauptmann Friedrich,' he bellowed.

Then the Hauptmann turned to me again. 'The name is Friedrich, Hauptmann Friedrich. Don't ever forget that name.'

For the next two weeks I cursed it — along with fifty other

recruits dressed, like me, in Army uniforms without any identifying tags. They were hard men, and they called themselves
Hitler's 'last known reserves'. The training was satanic. We had
an *Oberleutnant* resolved to prove his manhood at our expense.
As with most of the staff at Torgau he was mortally afraid of being
posted on active service, and this was his opportunity to show
how essential he was to the home front. The same kind of cowardice motivated guards at concentration camps. Fear is a powerful
spur.

While the Jews were victims of a racial madness, we were
subjected to treatment almost as harsh, as part of the Prussian
military code.

'On your knees, start digging,' the Oberleutnant yelled. Dig
with what? Then I saw the others scrabbling at the hard-packed
earth with their fingers. I started too.

We stopped when our fingers were bleeding — and not before.
We marched in full equipment with steel helmets and wooden
guns until our legs buckled beneath us; from eight in the morning
until five at night without ceasing, without food, or drink under a
relay of screaming, bawling instructors. When there had been
rain, and the parade ground was muddy, the order was 'On your
bellies, crawl.' And we did. For miles, edging forward on raised
elbows, hands clinging for dear life to our wooden rifles; to drop
these would mean an extra half-hour of torture. After ten days
three prisoners had hanged themselves from their bunk beds.
The Oberleutnant's only comment was to observe that it was a
pity we all hadn't followed suit. We were expendable; trash
whose sole purpose was to die for the Fatherland. This was
drummed into us every hour on the hour.

Sour grey bread and greasy tepid cabbage soup and acorn
coffee was my lot. Since I was on half-rations, I was 'excused'
breakfast.

After the end of two weeks I was ordered to report to Hauptmann Friedrich.

After the usual 'Jakob Kersten, sabotage and desertion,' he
said abruptly, 'Tomorrow you will be transferred to a 'special
commando.' That meant a death squad, a 'heaven-bound'
commando.

Forty of us gathered in the compound outside the west wing;
Feldwebel Günther in command. Before we were called to attention I whispered to my neighbour, 'Where the hell are we going?'

'We are going to Naumburg to dig unexploded bombs and defuse mines. I wish to God they'd finish us off here, the bastards.'

A command: 'Company, company atten-shun. Eyes to the front.' Feldwebel Günther reported to the approaching Friedrich: 'Company assembled for the Hauptmann's personal inspection.'

Friedrich stood before us: 'I have decided that all of you will volunteer for a special bomb-digging commando in Naumburg. So that every decent soldier will recognize you, you will wear a white strip of cloth on your right arm-sleeve carrying, in black letters, your description *Sonderabteilung* [special troop].

'However, if any of you present does not wish to volunteer, let him take one step forward. He will be allotted other duties.' No one stepped forward.

We marched off to the railway station in silence. By a special Führer decree we were forbidden to sing, being soldiers without honour. It is a fair guess that no one felt like singing.

On the station platform I participated in a little incident which in a way personified Germany at that time.

Our ten guards were all home-front soldiers without a decoration among them, even though none was over thirty-five.

An elderly woman approached, wearing a railway uniform: the ticket-collector, whom I recognised from my arrival at Torgau. Before the guards realized what she had in mind she handed two cigarettes to me.

'God bless you and save you, soldier,' she said softly.

'Get away, woman,' shouted one of the guards. 'You know it is forbidden to give anything to prisoners.' Feldwebel Günther dashed up and pushed the woman aside. 'Do you realize you could be sent to prison for what you have done?'

In rising anger the woman faced him: 'I have lost my two sons at the front. Both had won medals for gallantry. I see no medals on your chest.'

For a moment I thought Günther was going to assault her, then the station-master arrived. He planted himself in front of the Feldwebel with the absolute assurance of German bureaucracy. 'This woman,' he said, pointing to the ticket-collector, 'has given everything for Germany — her husband and two sons. Her home was bombed into rubble a few nights back. Keep away from her, Feldwebel, or I will have you reported for serious misconduct in public.'

Günther's eyes were fixed on the station-master's chest. Kaiser war ribbons and, much more important, the golden Nazi Party badge for long service; proof that the station-master had worked for the Party in the struggle for power prior to 1933.

Günther backed off — and took it out on me. 'I order you,' he said, 'to hand over these cigarettes.'

'You have enough of your own,' I answered.

'Prisoner, I must warn you, I have the right to shoot you for refusal to obey an order. I tell you once more: hand over the cigarettes or face the consequences.'

'You don't dare shoot me in public,' I responded, sensing his insecurity. 'You would find yourself on the Eastern Front.'

'For the last time,' he said, 'hand over the cigarettes or face another court-martial.'

I stretched out my hand and let the cigarettes fall to the ground.

'You bastard!' Then Günther put his heavy boot on them and ground them into the dirt.

So honour and authority were satisfied all round. The station-master took it out on the sergeant and the sergeant took it out on the prisoner and the prisoner took it out on the cigarettes. The hierarchy endured.

Within minutes of this illuminating exchange we were on our way to Naumburg, safely perched in two goods wagons, each with a small ventilation grille, criss-crossed with barbed wire. The guards had their own wagon.

Naumburg lies 100 kilometres from Torgau, a three-hour journey at the most. Due to bombings and troop movements, the journey lasted four days. We were diverted to a siding at Leipzig, and there we remained, locked in without food and water, choking on the smell of our excrement. Günther, it was reported, remarked that he hoped we would suffocate in our own filth.

At Naumburg we were marched — or rather we staggered — to Sportplatz 05, an athletics stadium converted into a prison compound. There we received double rations to make up for our lack of them under Günther.

The compound had high perimeter fences; Alsatian dogs prowled outside in a deep ditch; they were trained to kill. We were to be housed in wooden barracks where the windows were thickly covered with barbed wire. Our depression deepened still further after we had our first — and only — instruction about clearance. It was given by an Oberleutnant, and lasted exactly half an hour. We were then informed we were ready for action, which would begin next morning. We stripped and showered our stinking bodies and made for the bunks and sleep.

I had clambered into a top bunk when a fellow prisoner came across to me. He said that he was a spokesman for the group. 'I was a major in the Luftwaffe before I was arrested.' I had already noticed how the indefinable quality of leadership had singled him out: almost like a wolf-pack with its chosen chief.

'Strange things happen in this world, Dutchman. To us you are not a saboteur or a deserter, merely a prisoner.'

'Thank you, Major. I simply took a risk and it didn't come off. It backfired.'

He smiled. 'You are lucky. At least you know what you are here for. We' — he gestured vaguely, 'don't even know that. The military police, supported by the SS, arrested us only hours after Hitler had visited our air base in the Ukraine. We were supposed to have been part of a plot.[1] I reckon our chances of survival are slim. Our only hope is escape. If you get a chance, take it.' With that he walked off to his own bunk, leaving me wondering how many medals the gallant major had won, and what wretched misfortune had reduced him to the ranks of the 'heaven-bound'. His advice to escape seemed pretty superficial, and excessively optimistic.

Around 2 a.m. the sirens sounded. Naumburg's citizens took to their shelters. Naumburg's prisoners remained firmly locked in. We were expendable.

Thanks to the RAF there was no cooked breakfast in the morning. The cook had been on fire duty. So we had to make do with watery coffee substitute and go to work on the RAF's leavings on empty stomachs.

Each of us was provided with a shovel and pick, divided into sections of four and marched off. Large numbers of phosphorus canisters had been dropped to create the kind of firestorm which had devastated Hamburg some months previously, but this time they had not been notably successful. Indeed it had not been a particularly good night for the RAF: the proportion of unexploded bombs to the total dropped was unbelievably high. Despite

[1]For a period Hitler had his headquarters at Vinnitsa in the Ukraine. It is quite possible that rumours of plots (real or fictional) reached the SS from early 1943 onward. A number were indeed attempted, although those *recorded* were confined to Army elements on the Central Front.

that, there was still plenty of damage: the stench of burned flesh hung in the air over the rubble; signs declaring *Blindgänger*[1] were everywhere in evidence.

Our first target was the removal of unexploded bombs near a huge refrigerated food store. We were warned not to touch anything; not even scorched cheeses. Anyone caught with food was automatically charged with looting and executed. I noticed, however, that Party bigwigs frequently called for unharmed food.

I was paired off with another prisoner, Rudolf, and ordered to start digging for a bomb embedded in the foundation of a six-storey building. The guards, naturally, kept themselves well clear.

Some of the bombs were stuck deep in the earth. To defuse them we had first to free them. I stared at my first live bomb, and was simply paralysed with fright. I'd never known real fear before. Now my whole body shivered when my spade touched the metal of the bomb. I started to sweat. I cursed. I prayed. I couldn't breathe. I was waiting for the damn thing to blow up. Rudolf comforted me. 'My first time I cried like a child.' So the poor bastard had done a 'tour' before.

'Go on, Dutchman, touch the bloody thing.' So I touched it with my hand, and the feel of solid cold steel made me normal again.

Having dug round the bomb, we erected a derrick and placed two wire loops round the fins. Slowly, slowly, the bomb was raised from the hole; inch by inch it moved, till finally it swung free. The point of danger was when the three-metre cylinder was upright. When the winchman had swung the bomb away from the building the real experts got down to defusing the weapon.

Two days later things did not go so smoothly. A couple of blocks away a bomb went off. Four prisoners and a guard were killed: the segments of two prisoners could not be identified. A prisoner — a former lieutenant — gazed at the scrapings. 'For Führer and Fatherland, Sieg Heil.' He could not be charged for insubordination — anyway, the guards were in no mood to charge anyone — for the official Nazi declaration to next-of-kin was exactly that: 'died for Führer and Fatherland'. 'That's the trouble with digging up bombs,' remarked the ex-lieutenant as he turned away. 'You get careless after a while.'

---

[1]No way forward.

After five weeks our original commando of forty had been reduced to eighteen. No replacements were to be sent until we were all dead or incapacitated, an event which did not seem likely to be long delayed.

Yet there was even a slim — an almost impossibly slim — chance of regaining our honour and liberty. For every fifteen bombs we helped to render harmless, one year was taken off our sentence. For me that meant 225 bombs. At the rate I was digging them out, two or three a week, it might take a couple of years to clear my sentence. The Luftwaffe major reckoned the odds against that happening at about 1,000 to one.

He was expert on the German punishment system. He recalled how he and his unit, suspected of being implicated in this apparently mythical plot against Hitler (he certainly denied any knowledge of it) were initially selected for Torgau and 'special service'. The SS officer came round to each prisoner. 'How long?' 'Twelve years, Herr Sturmbannführer.' 'Very well. You're chosen.' Anyone with a sentence of ten years or more qualified.

The Luftwaffe major had a remarkably philosophic view of his fate.

He told me that when he and the others had formed into a Sonder Battalion they did four weeks' special service on the Eastern Front, and after that bomb-digging in Osnabrück. Of the original two hundred — 'there were seventeen left.'

The major and I had been talking in the dark — lights out was nine o'clock and it was now near midnight. Suddenly the wail of the siren roused everyone: the RAF were back.

We stayed in our bunks for there was nowhere for us to go. If we survived, well and good; we could go on digging out bombs: if we were killed, so be it. There were more where we came from. But then the drone of planes became louder and louder. The major leapt from his bunk — taking command came easy to him. 'Everyone up and dressed for emergency. This will be a big one.' At that moment the first wave of aircraft came over Sportplatz 05. They continued to come. The drone became louder; the explosions nearer. Fingers dug into the wooden floorboards, we waited for the inevitable. The walls shook, the floor quivered, the din was unbearable — and then peace. No more noise.

I raised my head and looked at a huge hole in the barrack wall: outside flames were eating the darkness — and the perimeter fence. As I scrambled to my knees I felt a hand on my shoulder.

The major said, 'Go on, Dutchman, don't wait. Get the hell out of here. You'll never get a better chance.'

'And you?'

'No, I have a wife and two children at home. They'd arrest the three of them and hold them till I returned. Anyway, I'm German. My place is here. But you go. Now.'

I scrambled to my feet and he grabbed my tunic: 'Here, take this jack knife. You'll need it for the dogs outside.' He was right.

Half-way to the smouldering wrecked fence, I heard a warning growl. Turning to the left, I could make out the eyes of an Alsatian.

The dog stared at me: his growls growing louder, heavier, more menacing. I bent my knees slightly to react that more swiftly. When the Alsatian decided to spring on me his eyes had risen in line with my throat. I could see the white fangs bared in a snarl. Then he jumped. As he did so I side-stepped, heard the snap of his jaws, felt the heat of his body as the hairs brushed my cheek. Automatically my hand flashed out, grabbing the animal's nearest hind-leg. A sickening sound of tearing sinew; a fearful howl and the dog's body hit the ground with a terrific thud. I slashed at it, and my knife went in to the hilt. Then I ran through the broken fence towards Magdeburg where I had contacts, my way lit by the flames of Naumburg.

Ten

The Paper Jacket

Life on the run was just as you picture it: lying up by day, in a copse, ditch or deserted barn; moving at night grabbing turnips or anything edible from the fields, while on two lucky occasions Polish farmworkers shared their rations with me.

I was making for Magdeburg because I had been told two Die Wasserkante members lived there (they didn't, as I was to discover: they'd been killed in air raids). My main problem was clothes. The prison garb was a complete give-away. Papers, that bane of living in a bureaucracy, were not so much of a worry in the early months of 1944 because Germany was now so saturated with bombing and consequent destruction of homes and contents that the excuse 'my papers have been burned' had become quite acceptable. One simply went to the nearest Party office to get a duplicate. Or in my case one couldn't. Which was why I was making for Günther and Sven in Magdeburg: to fit me up with forged documents.

As an attempt to elude my captors my prison escape wasn't bad, and it gave me a fascinating insight into life in Nazi Germany after four years of war. Some 15 kilometres from Magdeburg I spied a modest little farmhouse. I observed it closely all day, and finally decided to risk everything by asking the young resident Polish farmworker for old clothes. Like all his kind, he wore the large 'P' on his jacket. This was not only to aid German soldiers in identifying him (many Polish workers had little or no German) but to warn off Aryan women.

The Pole had no clothes to give me, and quite naturally did not want to risk his life helping an escaped prisoner. But, incredibly, his employer (I hesitate to use the word 'mistress' for, emphati-

cally, she was that only in the employment sense) took me in.
Frau Hildegarde was a dear, gentle, homely Christian woman.
On the Sabbath she read from the big, heavily padded Lutheran
bible, written in old German and, when not in use, carefully
covered with an embroidered cloth. She had lost her husband
and only son in Russia. She was lonely and generous-hearted:
telling the local, not very zealous, policeman who weekly checked
up on the behaviour of foreign farm labourers that I was a young
Dutch friend who had come to the countryside to escape the
bombing up north. She wanted to adopt me — not officially, of
course, but to keep me in a safe haven until the war was over.

I was sorely tempted, but eager to get on with my own war, so,
duly clad in a suit belonging to Frau Hildegarde's son, plus
money and luggage, I hitched a lift with a Flemish truck-driver
travelling to Magdeburg.

Magdeburg was just another flattened German city. My contacts had been killed. I was at my wits' end. I needn't have
worried, for I was recaptured within hours. Quite easily too.

In yet one more air-raid on that battered city I rescued a little
girl and took her to a hospital. I had been knocked unconscious
for a while myself, so I was a bit hazy about what I was doing. I
remember bits of torso showering round me as I staggered
through the streets and lifting up this tiny bundle, one of whose
legs was almost severed. I couldn't undestand why no one would
help me. There were plenty around. Then I noticed they were too
busy. Looting — and never mind about the punishment being
death.

Limping badly — I had also been injured in the knee — I finally
staggered to a hospital and promptly collapsed. When I came to
my left knee was swathed in bandages and my right arm was
manacled to the bed head. My neighbour in the next bed told me I
had been delirious, and talked in my sleep about my escape from
Torgau . . .

The development which astounded me was the arrival of
Hauptmann Friedrich; a *benign* Hauptmann Friedrich inquiring
after my health, referring to me, almost genially, as 'Herr Kollege'
and offering me a cigarette. I could not believe that his change in
attitude had been occasioned by the fact that I had rescued a
child, although I accepted that this act may have made me something of a local hero and could mitigate my sentence. Hauptmann
Friedrich reluctantly confessed that by sending me on bomb-

digging detail to Naumburg he had exceeded his authority.

'You see,' he said, 'you were classified as a high-risk prisoner who should not have been allowed outside the *Festung* at Torgau. I acted outside my jurisdiction.' The Hauptmann had transgressed the first law of Prussian militarism: *'Befehl ist Befehl'* (orders are orders). He was full, not of contrition, but of fear. He had falsified the records to protect himself, noting that I had escaped from Torgau, not Naumburg. Now he was as much in my power as I was in his. If I would assist him in concealing the truth he would try to get my sentence for escaping minimized, and do everything to make life easier for me in Torgau. There was just one snag. 'You will have to go through the appropriate procedure for escapees. That means you will have to return to Torgau in chains and spend several weeks in the,' — he paused — 'punishment block.' He paused again. 'Well, actually it is the death row, but I do assure you nothing will happen. After your hearing you will go back to routine duties, and as you are an experienced engineer I will be able to fix you up with something comfortable.'

I had no real choice. My fear was that Friedrich would simply eliminate me once he had me in Torgau, but then I calculated he would not dare do this with a specially classified prisoner (and I was sure that this was Inge's doing, thanks to her influence with 'Gestapo Müller'). Anything happening to me would prompt a swift and thorough investigation. I accepted his terms — and a packet of cigarettes.

The next four weeks were horrible beyond belief. The war had reached the stage — it was March 1944 — when the single slender hope for avoiding defeat (no one spoke with any conviction of 'victory') lay in the vengeance weapons to be launched against England. For the rest, a dread foreboding pressed down on the people. Punishment had replaced patriotism as the spur to duty.

Under the 'Commander Order' those in charge of divisional areas on the Russian front where towns were surrendered to the Soviets bore ultimate responsibility for capitulation, and were dealt with accordingly: demotion, imprisonment, even death. But the Führer's headquarters decided to pin responsibility on those who actually retreated from a strongpoint: brigade, battalion, down to company command. This vastly extended the number liable to be prosecuted for cowardice. I was to see what happened to the German victims of Hitler's 'No Withdrawal' policy, for Torgau Festung, as one of the oldest and most feared military prisons, was the natural last resting-place of those convicted of putting their own lives and those of their soldiers before Führer and Fatherland.

Duly re-established in Torgau — this time complete with wooden clogs to mark me as an escaper — I was locked into cell No. 4 on the ground floor of the east wing: the death row.

In the early hours of the following morning my cell door swung open and in the dimly lit corridor I could make out two guards. 'Prisoner, come forward.' One of them carried ankle fetters. I was ordered to turn round with my back to the guards while the fetters were fastened. My first and only thought was 'I am to be shot.' Outside in the corridor were two other prisoners, similarly shackled. No one spoke. We stared wild-eyed at each other. We were marched off to the end of the east wing. There stood six guards under command of a Feldwebel. Immediately behind them was a small door leading to the exercise yard.

We were told to remove our prison jackets and put on green paper jackets: the sure sign that one was to be executed — good uniforms were too scarce to be wasted. In the bitter cold I sweated freely; my hands and feet burned; my throat contracted as my glands swelled; I couldn't swallow or breathe properly, and my whole body shook uncontrollably.

One of the guards opened an adjacent cell. There stood a middle-aged man. Completely naked. He held his uniform neatly folded over one arm; all insignia had been removed, but a lighter patch near the collar suggested he was the holder of an Iron Cross. The man was ordered from his cell and made to stand opposite me. Suddenly I realized it was the naked man who was to be shot, not me. I would clothe him in the paper jacket. The whole business was a grisly charade.

I scrutinized the man who was about to die. Forty? Forty-five? High-bridged nose; quizzical blue eyes, misted over now as he fought to hold back memories and tears. Had he been a major or a colonel? Had he made the decision to retreat knowing his near-certain doom for the sake of his men or had this appalling sentence come to him as a complete shock? What kind of army had the German Wehrmacht become that it would condone or even encourage the execution of its own at the behest of a former corporal — and an Austrian corporal at that?

Even while these thoughts were passing through my mind the

guards were opening another cell. Again there stood a naked man, but he did not move. He was tall and well built, his eyes round and staring, and he just stood his ground as though he had not heard the command to step forward into the corridor. I noticed his right arm was badly mangled; the bones had been joined by a pin which protruded from beneath his flesh. Clearly a war wound.

The guards closed in on their prisoner, but they used soft, coaxing words: 'It's all right, friend. No one will hurt you.' The prisoner's body began to shake and saliva trickled down his chin. His hands clenched and his lips curled back in a half-scream. A brave man was being reduced to the level of a maddened animal. I expected him to go berserk at any moment, but he didn't: the two guards knew their business. They seized the prisoner by his thighs and under his armpits and threw him over the back of a third guard, laughing the while. But the third guard slipped and the prisoner sloughed off his back and fell to the floor with a sickening thud.

A high-pitched scream echoed through the corridors of Torgau Festung. The pin connecting the bone of his injured arm had broken and the limb flopped uselessly, held together only by the torn muscles.

One of the guards grinned and, pointing to the writhing man, remarked, 'Just two more after this one and I've shot myself four weeks' home leave all in one.'

The guards came out from the cell and one turned to me: 'You. Dress him.' My previous charge was dressed by another prisoner.

So I helped the convicted officer into his last uniform, the green paper jacket of death, and carefully left the broken arm hanging free. For this service he thanked me. His mood had changed from madness to childish tranquillity. Maybe he had made his peace. Maybe his mind had simply gone.

The two officers were led out into the exercise yard; I and another two prisoners detailed for execution duty followed a short distance behind, pushing a small hand cart which was used to wheel away the corpses.

The prisoner with the injured arm did not appear to understand what was happening. 'Just a short walk, old chap, and a doctor will look after you. Be careful now, son. Don't touch it,' murmured a guard of the other's arm, clearly anxious that there should be no last-minute breakdown in a well-ordered routine.

I never thought I would see a cold-blooded execution of German officers by volunteer German soldiers. Germans shooting Germans for the reward of half a day's home leave for each individual shot.

When it was over my two companions and I loaded the corpses into the cart. My stomach yawed at the sight of the torn flesh. I hadn't realized the cutting power of rifle-bullets.

I wondered about the guards. When — if ever — they faced a tribunal what would be their answer to the charge that they had acted as they had done? 'We were ordered to do so. We had no choice.' Yet they were volunteers. They enjoyed their work.

I wondered too when — if ever — the German Army would get rid of those who were ordering the murder of German officers and German honour.

Eleven

Enter Stauffenberg

The days in death row passed agonizingly slowly. I got accustomed to execution duties; became quite callous really. The victims were all German officers who regarded death by firing squad as honourable, so why should I shed tears? Except that I was becoming as mindless as the poor victim with his pinned arm.

I walked up and down my cell for hours on end; eight paces from one corner to the other . . . one turn repeat . . . repeat . . . repeat. I found myself shouting, 'Come on, get it over and done with, for heaven's sake.' I didn't even feel faint when, four weeks after being put in the death row, the cell door opened to reveal a sergeant accompanied by a guard carrying fetters and manacles. 'Come forward, prisoner, and chain your legs,' snapped the sergeant. He spoke in a cold, clipped voice. I stepped forward and bent to put the manacles round my ankles: this submission by humiliation always roused me to rage, but as this appeared to be the prelude to my execution I attempted, pathetically, to maintain my diginity. But then my mind reacted to the shock and I realized I was not being dressed for a killing but secured for a trial.

The hearing concerning my escape was held in Torgau's administrative block, and with what panoply! There were no fewer than six different banners on display.

On the table lay the Wehrmacht flag with the Iron Cross in the top corner; behind, draped against the wall stood the standards of the Army: white, with the black Maltese Cross for the infantry; red for the artillery; yellow for the cavalry; pink for the armoured troops and over all the Nazi Party banner of blood-red, white circle, black swastika. We went through the same pantomime with the prosecuting attorney acting as my defence counsel. I was amused to hear my killing of the Alsatian dog described as 'wilful destruction of Army property'. Then strangely the hearing took a 180 degree turn in my favour. The military policeman (normally the scourge of the ordinary fighting-man) narrated my 'heroism' in saving the little girl during the Naumburg air raid. His evidence was endorsed by a nun who had also witnessed the incident. 'He is a good young man,' she added in her effort to be helpful, 'who forfeited his freedom to save a young life thrust by God into his hands. He should be set free.'

This proved too much for the Herr Kriegsgerichtrat,[1] who remarked icily that 'while your plea for mercy will be taken into consideration, that mercy is not always justified'. Yet the sentence was unbelievably light: an extra two years' imprisonment, with right to appeal for clemency at the war's end. I was to be removed from death row immediately and returned to normal duties. Hauptmann Friedrich received a severe reprimand.

How extraordinary, I mused as I was led away, that the Germans should show such punctilious regard for justice at one moment and hang you without regard for it at the next.

During the course of the hearing I noticed the Court President refer again and again to my file, and especially to the letter stamped with the SS emblem and marked *Geheim*; Inge's good-luck charm to me. When, shortly afterwards, I was brought before Hauptmann Friedrich I noticed that he too paid particular attention to this document — and then offered me a position 'in the organization', so to speak. If I wished I could become heating engineer-in-chief for Torgau! He was keeping his side of the deal struck in Magdeburg. As heating engineer (Torgau had a superb heating system) I would be free to go anywhere in the prison unless specifically forbidden. I would report only to Hauptmann Friedrich.

Suddenly I was 'somebody' in the hierarchy, and in terms of the prison community a very important somebody: the skilled man, the technician.

With responsibility came authority, and with authority came power: even in prison — perhaps more so in prison — the Nazi/Prussian philosophy of total command prevailed. A young Panzer lieutenant was assigned to me. He was a former member

[1]War Court Judge: usually a major.

of the Hitler Jugend, a full Party member from Gelsenkirchen, a real Nazi fanatic, who had fallen foul of his military commander and been sent to Torgau. When I told him to clean some steel plates he replied flatly that a Panzer lieutenant didn't take orders from a 'blasted foreigner'. I beat him up. Savagely. I had adjusted to the system.

One who witnessed the thrashing silently and pensively was a middle-aged major who had dared question his colonel's passion for music. The Colonel, in the Vth Corps in the Caucusus, had insisted on soldiers being consigned from front-line duties to guard musical instruments. Taking his colonel to task proved an expensive piece of insubordination for the major. He was sentenced to ten years for disobeying an order in a fighting zone. '*Befehl ist Befehl* . . .'

To conform with the German passion for symbols and titles, I wore a white armband with the letter 'H' for *Heizung* (heating) emblazoned on it. My success in restoring full central heating — pressure had fallen drastically because the pipes had not been properly cleaned for four years — brought me further prestige. Gates opened automatically at my approach. One day, as I went about my tasks, an officer prisoner — a major, actually — stopped me and asked me in a sharp authoritative tone, 'What exactly does that stand for?' pointing to the armband. Without hesitation I answered, 'Kommandant für Heizung, Herr Major.'

Instantly he drew himself to attention and saluted me.

'If it stands still, paint it: if it moves, salute it.' I recalled the old saying, common to all armies. But probably only in the German Army would one salute a central-heating engineer.

By an incredible chain of circumstances I was now to witness the transformation of Torgau into an anti-Hitler bastion and a key element in the plot to oust the Führer. The limping Dutchman with his clogs (for the badge of the escapee remained) was to observe and not to be observed. I was part of the furniture at Torgau. That is why I survived.

*   *   *

Some of what follows is based on long talks with General Oskar von Niedermayer when he was in Torgau from the end of September 1944 until April 1945. Although Die Wasserkante did not participate in the plot against Hitler, Niedermayer was in contact with those generals who were involved — as with those who opposed, and actually betrayed — the coup. We have also called on many other original written sources — von Herwarth, von Schlabrendorff, Otto John, as well as secondary accounts of the attempted coup.

Die Wasserkante had decided, as already mentioned, to take no action alongside the resistance generals because of the fundamental difference in aims. But Niedermayer knew of every move being made by the conspirators.

It was the dream of Klaus von Stauffenberg which became the driving force of the conspirators. This classically handsome colonel had been brutally mutilated in a North African minefield, losing his left eye, right hand and two fingers of his left hand. At thirty-six he was a physical wreck, but his wounds had served to fire his raging wrath against Hitler, the Nazis and the war.

General von Tresckow — he who had attended the meeting with Die Wasserkante — selected Stauffenberg to be chief administrator of the plot, following the failure of previous attempts to eliminate Hitler.

Stauffenberg, having sufficiently recovered from his wounds, had insisted on returning to duty, and in June 1943 had been promoted colonel and, given his injuries, allowed a certain latitude in his military duties.

In August Stauffenberg launched himself on a remarkable endeavour: no less than to recruit the field commanders of the Wehrmacht to a conspiracy to overthrow Adolf-Hitler, their Supreme Commander, to whom they had sworn an oath of allegiance. It is a measure of the extraordinary prestige enjoyed by an aristocratic General Staff officer in the German Army — and to the extent of the disaffection — that there could be such an attempt.

The coup was to be called 'Valkyrie' — a tribute, no doubt, to the Führer's well-known love for the works of Richard Wagner. The clever thing about Valkyrie was that it could be used as a cover for perfectly legitimate contingency planning.

German field commanders, military governors, chiefs of rear echelon troops, were acutely aware of the possibility of an SS coup to put more power into the hands of Nazi zealots such as SS Reichsführer Heinrich Himmler. *Der Führer* might indeed require protection from his praetorian guard. Had not the Brownshirt leaders — the original Nazi élite — been brutally suppressed in 1934 to ensure Hitler's concordat with the Wehrmacht? So might not the same medicine be administered to the SS, the infinitely more powerful successors to the Brownshirts?

If such plans were to be partially leaked (the detailed preparations were held by General von Tresckow's wife Erika, who had carefully copied them out for each command, and by another plotter, General Olbricht), they could therefore be explained as sensible protective measures. In the Byzantine atmosphere of Nazi Germany it would be considered quite natural for one segment of the State — the Army — to take precautions against another — the Party's uniformed élite — for the Führer's protection, of course. Moreover, Operation Valkyrie had a still more innocent outer cover. The plan could be used to deal with an uprising of foreign workers, of whom there were many millions in Germany. Army commanders could be ordered, on receipt of the code word 'Valkyrie', to round up *whomsoever the sealed orders designated*. They would not necessarily know the full extent of their actions. Nor certainly would the soldiers, whose loyalty was still unswervingly to their Führer. Only the inner core of conspirators were aware of the key proclamation to be issued over the signature of Field Marshal Erwin von Witzleben announcing the death of the Führer, and the Army's assumption of power.

During other murder attempts which misfired Stauffenberg went on laying his careful groundwork for the replacement of the Nazi regime by a new Germany. The vital factor was communications: if Rastenburg, the Wolf's Lair, the Führer's headquarters in the dark forests of East Germany, could be totally cut off from contact with Berlin, while the Army's HQ in Berlin's Bendlerstrasse were free to contact every German Army command, then even if fate did spare the Führer yet again, Operation Valkyrie could still go ahead with a fair chance of success.

Next in importance to communications came the attitude of operational Army commanders, and so Stauffenberg visited a number of the top brass of the Wehrmacht. The response was hardly encouraging. Men like von Rundstedt, von Manstein, Heinz Guderian, would not betray the conspirators — at least, not then — but would have nothing to do with toppling the Führer. This had little to do with loyalty to National Socialism: they just thought the whole idea crackpot, and a slur on German military honour.

Among German generals in the West a better climate prevailed. The military commandant in Paris, General von Stuelpnagel — a remarkably cool customer — was wholly in favour, and confident that his soldiers would act swiftly and mercilessly against the SS (whom they disliked violently). The military commandant in Belgium, von Falkenhausen, was another enthusiast for the coup. Field Marshal Rommel was an enigma. The most heroic and popular military figure in Germany since Hindenburg was not convinced that everything was lost. He owed his Field Marshal's baton to Hitler. He owed his command of the field armies which would oppose the Allied armies invading France from across the Channel to Hitler. This chivalrous and splendid soldier — to whom Winston Churchill paid tribute in the House of Commons across the gulf of war — would not become part of the conspiracy. And yet . . . he permitted conspiracy to be hatched at his own headquarters, a fact which condemned him to death a year later.

In this autumn of 1943 the war was closing in on the Reich. Italy had surrendered following its invasion by Montgomery's Eighth Army. On the Eastern Front the Germans had been driven back relentlessly. Kiev and almost all the Ukraine was lost. The commander of the East central front, Field Marshal Günther von Kluge, was brought round by the evidence of catastrophe to condone the conspiracy. 'If Hitler dies, count on me.' Such was his response, and that of a number of others, not least the commander of the Home Army: the heavy-featured, piggy-eyed General Friedrich Fromm.

Having taken the reins into his own hands, evolved the Valkyrie cover, made the rounds of senior sympathizers and winnowed the lukewarm from the committed, Klaus von Stauffenberg resolved that a final date must be set when the conspiracy would go ahead regardless. Germans, he argued, must free Germany from tyranny. On 24 May 1944, Empire Day, Mr Churchill told Parliament:

> We shall fight on together until Germany is forced to capitulate and until Nazism is extirpated. . . . I have repeatedly said that unconditional surrender gives the enemy no rights *but relieves us of no duties*. Justice will have to be done, and retribution will fall upon the wicked and the cruel. The miscreants who set out to subjugate first Europe and then the world must be punished.

In Germany the conspirators instantly took heart. Was not Churchill distinguishing between the guilty and the innocent? Surely now was the time to strike, before the Allies invaded France (an event expected daily), suffered the inevitably heavy casualties and became less understanding of one kind of German as against another? Stauffenberg disagreed with this analysis, expressing the view that the Western Allies were too cowardly to attack in 1944, and that if they did their losses might make them more ready, not less, to negotiate peace with a non-Nazi Germany.

Nevertheless, every segment of the conspiracy: military, political, pro-East, pro-West, was at one in agreeing that the time had come. The decisive factor was Stauffenberg's appointment at the end of June 1944 to be Chief of Staff to General Fromm's Home Army. For this post gave the real if unacknowledged leader of the conspiracy *direct access to the Führer*. No longer would the plotters need to wait on Hitler to come to them. Their man would now regularly attend the Führer's noon-day conference to report on developments within the Home Army.

Quite suddenly circumstances combined to point to mid-July 1944.

A series of cataclysmic military blows rained down upon Germany. One result of the Allied breakthrough in Normandy was that an enraged Führer on 2 July, dismissed his supreme commander in the West, Field Marshal von Rundstedt, and appointed Günther von Kluge in his place.

Here was a potent breakthrough for the conspirators. Rundstedt was cynical about Germany's chance but would in no circumstances condone a coup, let alone the murder of Hitler. He was no Nazi; he was simply a soldier who had given his oath. Kluge was a horse of a different hue altogether. High-domed, pale-eyed and rather shifty-looking, he was far from popular with his fellow-chieftains (Guderian, for example, hated him), but he was tepidly in favour of the conspiracy.

The 'new government' had already secretly been drawn up with General Ludwig Beck as Chief of State, Dr Carl Goerdeler as Chancellor, C-in-C of the armed Forces Erwin von Witzleben, and Klaus von Stauffenberg as State Secretary for War. Many other posts were filled by members of the old pre-Nazi parties: Socialist, Catholic Centre, Nationalist. The communists had not been forgotten. A special conference was convened between Julius Leber, the leading socialist in the conspirators' shadow administration (he was to be Minister of the Interior) and three communists in East Berlin to create a common front. Franz Jacob, the principal communist, remarked, 'The time has come to make a pact with the devil himself.' Die Wasserkante, however, held aloof.

Then a remarkable thing happened. The communists and socialists were betrayed. On 4 July those who had attended the meeting were arrested. Who betrayed them? An agent of the Gestapo who had infiltrated the communist organization? Or an agent of Stalin who intended to ensure that there would be no precipitate peace which would deny Russia the fullest fruits of victory? Either answer is possible. What is certain is that the arrest of Julius Leber, a close friend of Stauffenberg's and at the centre of the conspiracy, made immediate action imperative.

On 6 July Stauffenberg sent word to General von Tresckow, the major plotter on the Eastern Front: 'Expect action any day now.'

But action from whom? Whom could the conspirators trust to act? Well, for a start they had no known body of troops on whom they could rely. They had therefore to look to senior officers, and hope that the men these commanded would follow the orders of their leaders.

In Berlin, however, there was a fair-sized and strategically placed group including the military commandant of Berlin, General von Hase, most of the staff of General Fromm's Reserve Army and the police chiefs, Helldorf and Nebe. Everything hinged on communications: to isolate the Führer's headquarters at Rastenburg in East Prussia and free the Bendlerstrasse headquarters of the Army in Berlin, to issue instructions for Valkyrie throughout the Reich and occupied territories. In the *Nacht und Nebel* — the night and fog of doubt, obscurity and division — anything could happen; certainly the prospects of the conspirators would be vastly enhanced.

So far as communications were concerned, the conspirators were well served at the top. The chief Signals officer in Berlin, General Fritz Thiele, was one of their band and, more importantly, so was General Erich Fellgiebel, head of the Army's Communications Department in the Wolf's Lair, Hitler's HQ. If they were supported by a sufficiently strong team of experts and Wehrmacht technicians, then the 'coup by telephone', to use Goebbels's phrase, would have an odds-on chance of success.

However, the other side — the anti-conspirators — were skilled, still more alert to the importance of communications. Indeed, it was a reading of signal traffic which first stirred fears of a massive anti-Nazi conspiracy within the higher reaches of the German Army. Faulty conclusions were drawn from flawed data, and by one of the incredible blunders suspicions were aroused for the wrong reasons. But they were aroused. They looked for a conspiracy that didn't exist, but because they were looking — and at the communications establishment especially — they stumbled on the key role which Torgau had to play in the conspiracy. The role that has not until now been revealed, and the frustration of it was to doom the plot and the plotters.

Twelve

Voice of Honour

During June 1944 the conspirators in the Home Army — which had general surveillance over military prisons within the Reich — carefully concentrated technical and communications experts at Torgau. I saw too a change in the guards. The craven creatures who practised sadism to atone for cowardice were replaced by front-line soldiers whose wounds entitled them to rear-line echelon. Of course, I had no idea what this portended. I merely observed and noted.

Then on the afternoon of 17 July I witnessed the unbelievable: the cell doors were open. Most of the prisoners were standing in the corridors, chatting or walking up and down, heads thrown back: here and there the odd monocle gleaming. An air of intense expectancy gripped the entire prison as I eagerly invented work on the central-heating system that would take me to every corner of the fortress. I was in the north wing when I absorbed a murmur, rustling as the wind through these grey, melancholy passages. At first I could not make any sense of the whispered remarks. But after it had been repeated often enough it became clear: von Hofacker is here . . . von Hofacker is here . . . Von Hofacker is here . . . it is time at last!

Every prisoner leaned forward over the railings, looking in the direction of the south wing. I stood at the very end of the gangway, clear of everyone else. It was difficult to see what was going on, for the ground floor of the south wing was always in semi-darkness. I distinguished a movement, shadows in the gloom, voices rising in anticipation. And finally figures walking into full daylight of the centre of the prison. There were five of them: senior German officers.

My eyes focused on the central figure, now framed in the space between two wide steps of the staircase of the north wing. I recognized him immediately. He was Caesar von Hofacker, a Luftwaffe colonel attached to the Oberbefehlshaben West, the high command of the forces fighting the Allied invasion under the leadership of Field Marshal von Kluge, 'der kluge Hans.'[1]

It seemed that all the prisoners — who had by now eagerly seized every vantage point — knew Hofacker by sight. He seemed to be the leader, although from their insignia I could see that three of the other four outranked him. But then Caesar von Hofacker could out-talk the loftiest — which was why he was the leading figure.

I remembered him when we had met in Berlin. He looked the same: a dashing slim figure in his forties, of medium height, firm in his stride and exuding energy and charm.

As ever he was impeccably dressed, a walking advertisement for tailor-made clothing: this was not surprising, as he had been a wealthy industrialist before the war, and could afford the best from the finest tailors in either Berlin or Paris. Hofacker held his military hat, in regulation style, under his left arm. On his left breast was the Iron Cross 1st Class — he seemed the very picture of what Churchill had once proclaimed as 'the dandified, heel-clicking Prussian officer'.[2]

I knew others admired his ability to be discreet, reserved and level-headed. From my own observations I had learned that he was a man to be watched: too smooth, too polished — like his boots.

I recalled Hans, Die Wasserkante elder, revealing his own assessment of Hofacker, when we had met for the last time in Davoserstrasse in Berlin in June 1943: 'He is a master of words, a conductor of genius, using his gestures to orchestrate his argument, but he does it to mask his objectives. Believe me, he is a man without mercy. He has just one ambition in life: power.'

On Hofacker's left and slightly behind him stood the sharp-featured, bespectacled Captain Graf Schwerin von Schwanenfeld, the main liaison officer between Die Wasserkante and the military plotters. His beliefs were not the same as Hofacker's. Schwanenfeld was an 'Easterner' — anxious to make terms with

[1]'Clever Hans.' Hans was Günther von Kluge's second name, *Kluge* means 'clever'.

[2]Radio speech of 22 June, 1941.

Russia, ready to make peace in the West too, of course, but not willing to do so at the expense of the Soviets. He had supported Hans and General Niedermayer at the June conference, but Schwanenfeld's proposals had been swept aside by Hofacker, who insisted on war *à l'outrance* in the east while negotiating a settlement with the Anglo-Americans. Hans said of Schwanenfeld, who resembled a priest rather than a soldier, 'There is one who is absolutely sincere. A man whose word you can trust.'

The three other officers I had never seen before, but I overheard their names mentioned freely by my fellow-prisoners who were now craning over the balustrade to get a better view. One of the officers was General Fritz Thiele, second-in-command of the Technical Corps of the Reserve Army, stationed in Berlin: a Signals expert. The second was the Reserve Army's Inspector-General Carl von Thüngen; the third was the acting Chief Judge of the Army, Dr Carl Sack. All five were talking among themselves. I looked at them, shook myself, and said aloud, 'It's really happening. The putsch really is happening.' My neighbour said, 'Yes, he is here today to speak.'

He referred to Hofacker. This was the new Messiah, just as Hitler had been. I wondered if the unrepentant Nazis (such as my young Panzer lieutenant) had been removed from here to another prison — very probably they had. No one questioned orders: certainly not Hauptmann Friedrich, who as far as I could see was nowhere about.

Ironically, with the exception of the Hofacker contingent, I was almost certainly the only man in Torgau at that moment who fully understood, and was able to analyse, the real strength, inner disputes and likely prospects of the plotters and their bold move to take over Hitler's Germany.

Movement . . . General von Thüngen and Hofacker stepped forward a few paces. Both men were warmly applauded, the clapping echoing down the corridors. If this could happen in the most formidable military prison in Germany what was happening in the rest of the country?

Schwanenfeld and his companions moved back into the shadows.

There stood von Hofacker, silently, but already totally in command. He drew the eyes of every prisoner to him as a magnet attracts iron filings. The strange aura of leadership encompassed him. Once again the German yearning to worship and obey was being fulfilled. This was a lone figure, possessed of a dream, and willing to gamble his own life as well as that of others in the conspiracy. Now the whole population of Festung Zinna, Torgau — able, dedicated, superb technicians who had fallen foul of the SS or time-serving seniors, or had retreated from hopeless positions, were at one in wanting an end to a regime that was turning Germany into a cemetery.

I gazed long and deeply at the rows of prisoners, filling the landings, filling the staircases — testifying, as nothing else could, to the huge influx of new arrivals. I could see, in detail, their reactions. All faces were turned towards the Leader. Their eyes never left him. It was eerily reminiscent of the old newsreels of the Führer addressing the faithful.

As the last mutterings died away von Hofacker raised his hand, partly in salute, partly as a mute, imperious call for silence. He got it, and he began to speak: 'Comrades . . . officers of the German Army, I have come here specially today to address you as a fellow-officer and compatriot.'

These anodyne phrases created an electric atmosphere. Only a few words, yet already pride was shining in men's eyes. The prisoners, all former officers, looked across the landing at each other, nodding their heads, smiling as if they were confirming each other's thoughts. 'You see, we are needed after all . . . he has called us comrades.'

Von Hofacker continued, 'You will be aware that everywhere at the front we are being forced to stand and fight to the last man. On Hitler's irresponsible orders there is to be no surrender — no matter how hopeless the situation.

'In this way we have lost not only a great many of our experienced soldiers but also officers; officers who cannot be replaced in the short term. Against the better judgement of the General Staff and Army Commanders Hitler has continued on this criminal path. Anyone who dares to criticize his methods, or even use personal initiative, is relieved of his command immediately after being charged, like yourselves, with neglect of duty. Too often the court-martial's verdict is death.'

Von Hofacker paused. His timing was perfect. His audience was spellbound, and as he looked round the sea of faces he could gauge the remarkable reaction his words were producing. The Great Man was saying what they had thought so long and had not dared voice.

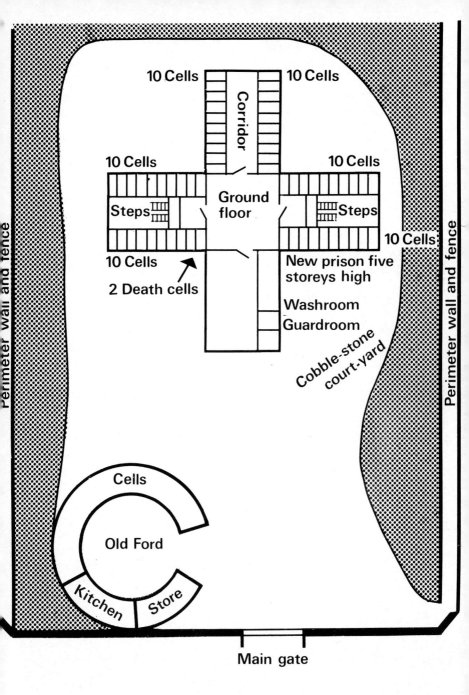

The layout of the prison at Torgau as drawn from memory by Jakob Kersten.

The author in 1967.

General Oskar von Niedermayer. Nicknamed 'the German Lawrence of Arabia', this erstwhile friend of Trotsky was a secret member of *Die Wasserkante,* a left-wing German resistance organisation.

Erwin Rommel: the severe wounds he received three days before the attempted *coup* put him in hospital during the crucial hours.

Field Marshal von Kluge, the vacillating commander in Paris who committed suicide on his recall to Berlin.

Heinz Guderian, the dashing Panzer Commander who was promoted to Chief of the Army General Staff hours after the attempt on Hitler's life. Did he betray the secret of Torgau?

He resumed. 'Some of our top field marshals — including Rommel, whom we all respect as a magnificent soldier — have requested Hitler to consider his own retirement. They have explained to him that, if he agrees, consideration would be given by certain powers to release orders that would end the senseless bombings and destruction of our cities.[1]

'This Hitler has flatly refused to consider. He will not listen to reason. Instead he has ordered a stepping up of the war effort. Now I can tell you that the Army commanders in the East and the West have decided, after lengthy discussions with civilian leaders, to take action to stop this wastage of German men and resources.

'We as officers ourselves, are fully aware that you are bound by your oath to obey the commanding authority. We are not asking you to break your oath, for your oath is to protect your wife, children and Germany. It is an oath not to be taken to one person only. Hitler's personal oath is to protect Germany. He is destroying her. We must destroy him now.' He gave these final words extra force and significance.

I looked at my neighbours: men who had nothing to lose and so much to gain. Some looked stunned. 'My God,' I thought, 'this is the way Hitler came to power, going from strength to strength on speech after speech.'

Again Hofacker's strong, confident voice broke out: 'The general command of the Army has carefully prepared itself over the past two months for a take-over of power by force. As you must be aware, this take-over is supported by well-known generals. You have seen some of them here with me today. Many of you assembled here have served under these commanders in successful campaigns in the east, west and south.'

Von Hofacker hesitated for perhaps ten seconds, then stretched his arms high, fists clenched: 'We have no alternative. We must act now. Not only to save the German Army from undeserved defeat, but to save our wives and families, our children who belong to the Germany of tomorrow. It is our duty as officers to safeguard Germany and secure it for them.'

He had finished. He let his arms fall to his side. He remained where he was standing, stock-still. He was indicating to his audience that it was for them to choose.

[1]Not true, albeit an understandable untruth. But for the Rommel position see page 101.

The silence following his address was so intense that I felt the hairs bristle at the back of my neck. I began to wonder if his stirring call had been in vain. He was clearly awaiting acknowledgement of his speech. Yet still this palpable quietness continued.

Then I heard a single cry from a prisoner only a few metres from me. The prisoner was tall and broad-shouldered with a round, rather innocent face, blue-eyed and fair haired: a true Aryan. His cry echoed round Festung Zinna. '*Es lebe Deutschland!* — Long live Germany!' As if in answer, another prisoner, somewhere in the east wing, began to sing the German National Anthem in a deep, melodious voice . . . '*Deutschland, Deutschland über alles.*'

Near to tears myself — and I hated German militarism — I could well imagine the effect on my fellow-inmates who still loved their army, its honour and their country. Around me men were joining in the singing, tears starting from their eyes and in some cases coursing down their cheeks. It was a fantastic, engulfing display of love for their Fatherland.

Then it was over The prisoners of Torgau had given their answer to Caesar von Hofacker. They were now waiting for him to tell them what part they were to play in the conspiracy. For their part they were committed — to the bitter end.

Hofacker remained motionless, clearly deeply moved by the response he had evoked. He looked upward to the high ceiling as though seeking spiritual inspiration.

Slowly he lowered his head, looking first to the right, then to the left, back to the centre. He started to speak again: 'Comrades . . . fellow-prisoners beware! Not all agree to our plans.' Each word was so carefully and deliberately pronounced that every prisoner must have been aware of the import.

'Most of those in the Armed Forces who do not support us are, of course, Party members. They should not be among our ranks but they were forced upon us. It is very noticeable that these men generally have comfortable, home-front postings.'[1] Here Hofacker raised his voice to fresh passion: 'Comrades, these men will attempt to hold on to power using any means available: a power given to them on the strength of their party membership

---

[1]Untrue. The fiercest fighting units were often composed of Nazi zealots — Hitler Jugend and Waffen SS formations. However, it was in the circumstances a pardonable mis-statement.

card. We are not in a position to withdraw fighting men from the front; something which I know you, as officers, will understand. But if our plans are to succeed these Nazi parasites must be isolated. And that is where we need your help.'

So this was it. We waited, scarcely breathing.

'In forty-eight hours from now two officers from the Reserve Army headquarters will come to Torgau. They will bring with them the actual instructions and will lead you throughout the take-over.

'You will be taken to Berlin in motor convoy, which will also carry the weaponry you need. From that moment, comrades, you are part of the take-over authority.

'Your role will be one to be proud of. You will hold the key to our success.' He paused. 'Your main task will be in line with your original training. You will secure all Army communication centres, including the chief one at Zossen on the outskirts of Berlin, and all main radio and telephone exchanges. We must prevent any damage as they must be fully operational by 12.00 hours on 20 July.'

At that moment Generals Thiele and von Thüngen re-entered. They stopped just short of von Hofacker, who on hearing their approach turned sharply, irritated at this interruption. Seconds passed. He resumed, with the message all the prisoners had been waiting for.

'After the transfer of power the new authorities will, by special decree, restore you to your former rank and return the decorations for valour which have been wilfully taken from you. The past will be forgotten and its files will be destroyed. You will be re-instated where you truly belong — leading the men of a free German Army.'

With these words a tumult of cheering broke out.

Von Hofacker raised his right hand, and silence fell once more on Festung Zinna. 'Soldiers of the German Army, comrades, fellow-officers, the people of Germany will be waiting and listening for your words. The success of the take-over is in your hands. Long live a free Germany!'

Once more a roar of cheering (how like a Party rally!) from the men who had faced ruin, perhaps death, and now lived again. The moment they had hoped, wept and prayed for had arrived at last.

I heard pledges of undying support; assurances showered on

the three officers standing together in this blaze of glory. They stood to attention and in turn each saluted the prisoners. Then walking slowly backward, they each raised one arm high in tribute to the 1,200 men who were to help liberate Germany. Then they were gone.

Around me small groups formed. And instructors, presumably from the outer fringe of the conspiracy, moved among them, briefing these forgotten prisoners of Torgau. Everyone spoke freely, naming names and places and leading personalities. I flitted from the edge of one group to another, overhearing what was being said. No one paid any attention to me. Security simply did not exist because no one saw the need for it.

I memorized the names I heard — von Witzleben, von Stuelpnagel, Fellgiebel, Beck, von Hase, von Treskcow, von Sponeck. There were also other names of lesser rank — von Hofacker, von Schwanenfeld and Stauffenberg. Then I thought about the towns I had heard mentioned. It struck me that each one had a military prison fairly near at hand, and also contained *Sonderbataillonen*, special units, composed of 'enemies of the regime', such as I had served with at Naumburg.

This combination of names clearly indicated how completely the generals were depending for success on the goodwill and co-operation of disaffected soldiers. I had no doubt, from my own experience, that they were absolutely right to do so. Such soldiers were ideal for the task, for they were willing to accept the generals' authority, and had proved themselves as brave fighting men in the field.

As I pondered on the remarkably careful planning which seemed to have gone into the preparation of the coup I heard the sound of heavy trucks approaching. Peering through a broken pane, I saw large military vehicles approaching the Festung yard from the direction of the main gate. I watched them closely as they drove past. I counted twenty-two of them, half with trailers. They were parked behind the east and west wings, completely hidden from view of the main gate.

So Hofacker's first promise — to provide transport — had been fulfilled. I noticed that the prisoners had been issued with the swastika eagle for their caps and tunics, re-establishing the official State insignia so that their appearance would cause no suspicions.

The prospects were brightening by the hour . . .

*   *   *

On this same 17 July the nascent coup suffered a shattering setback. Erwin Rommel's car was strafed by a British Mosquito aircraft and the Field Marshal gravely wounded.

Rommel himself was not in the conspiracy to kill Hitler, but he was prepared to surrender his armies in the West to General Eisenhower in order to end the senseless slaughter of his soldiers.

He had spoken of this with his staff, which included General Hans Speidel, who was in the plot, and he had already 'tested the water' for a general truce by arranging a three-hour armistice to permit the exchange of German women auxiliaries captured at Cherbourg for Allied wounded.

Four weeks after the D-day landings it had become incontestable that the Allies were going to break out and sweep the German armies from France. The VI bombardment had failed to halt the expansion of the bridgehead. The skies above the battlefield belonged wholly to the Allies. Faced with certain defeat in the West, and justifiably fearful that the colossal Russian victory in the East could bring the Soviet armies to Berlin, Rommel could see only one way out: peace in the West and continued struggle in the East, the very aim of the majority of the plotters.

For three days, 12, 13 and 14 July, Rommel toured the front, then he returned to his headquarters, sat down and wrote a message to the Führer.

In sharp, staccato phrases, reminiscent of his dashed-down dispatches in the rollicking years of victory, Germany's favourite soldier informed the man whom he had once worshipped that the war in the West was lost.

'The troops', he wrote, 'are fighting heroically everywhere, but the unequal struggle is nearing its end . . . It is, in my opinion, necessary to draw the appropriate conclusions from this situation without delay. I feel it is my duty as Commander-in-Chief of the Army Group to express this clearly.'

To Hans Speidel, his closest colleague, he remarked, 'I have given him [Hitler] his last chance. If he does not take it, we will act.'[1]

Speidel was close to the heart of the conspiracy, yet he apparently did not tell Stauffenberg, Beck and the others of Rommel's

[1]*Invasion Germany*, 1949, by Hans Speidel.

intended action. Why not? Did he mean to do so when he heard that Rommel had been wounded near to death and decided that no purpose could be served? The 'Easterners' distrusted Speidel. They were sure that he wanted a deal with Britain and America at the expense of the Soviet Union. They also doubted his complete identification with the cause, considering him to be a man with a foot in both camps: the conspiracy and the non-aligned.

This, it is said, could explain Speidel's readiness to encourage Rommel's unilateral action without informing the central conspirators, some of whom might have been opposed to it.

What if Rommel had offered Eisenhower a cease-fire in the West and German withdrawal to the Rhine? The Field Marshal could have carried the bulk of his soldiers with him. He had the approval of his own commander, von Kluge, who endorsed the dispatches Rommel sent to Hitler.

True the allies were pledged not to negotiate a separate peace. But surrender or agreed withdrawal on one front could not be said to constitute a negotiated peace.

General Eisenhower would certainly have been obliged to consult and take instructions from his political masters, President Roosevelt and Mr Churchill. Roosevelt was an implacable advocate of unconditional surrender; Churchill much less of one as his speeches in the House of Commons make plain. Roosevelt admittedly carried more weight, as the USA was in 1944 contributing the greater part of Allied material, and would soon supply the majority of soldiers. Nevertheless, 1944 was an election year in the USA and no President would wish to enter the contest accused of needlessly sacrificing 'American boys' when the enemy commander had offered to end the fighting and make way for the Allies' advance, at least to the German frontier.

Stalin, naturally, would have demanded the simultaneous surrender of German armies in the East (which would certainly not have taken place), but at that stage of the war his threats to sign a separate peace if he did not get his way would not have carried conviction. The Western Allies were well on the way to winning the war on their own — and the atomic bomb was just over the horizon.

Such speculation undoubtedly exercised many minds on the German side. Rommel's dallying with the enemy convinced Niedermayer that he had been right all along to stand aloof from the plot, and Stauffenberg, von Schwanenfeld and their 'Eastern' associates who looked for an all-round peace, embracing Russia, cannot have been too upset at the news of Rommel's injury. This remained true even though this injury robbed them of the one man who could have countered the still-magnetic force of Adolf Hitler.

At any rate, regardless of Rommel's moves and motivations in the West, Stauffenberg was now embarked on the active campaign to eliminate Hitler.

He took a bomb along to the Führer's midday conference at Berchtesgaden — Hitler's home in the Bavarian Alps — on 8 July and again on 11 July but decided against planting it as neither Himmler nor Goering were present. The plotters wanted to liquidate the second most powerful man of the Reich, Heinrich Himmler, thereby depriving the SS of their leader. Similarly, if Hermann Goering were disposed of it would rob the Nazis of one of their more popular politicians.

But when Stauffenberg got the call to present himself at the Führer's headquarters in the Wolf's Lair at Rasterburg on 20 July he resolved that regardless of who else was present Hitler must die, and that come what may, the coup must go ahead.

Thirteen

Operation Valkyrie

Dawn on 20 July presaged another hot, humid day. The sky was already glazed over in a brassy hue, when Klaus von Stauffenberg took the road to the Wolf's Lair at Rastenburg. He was accompanied by his aide, Werner von Haeften. It was, he felt, to relieve the German people of a pitiless sacrifice in an unrighteous cause that he must undertake his mission of murder.

But was that the only reason? According to Niedermayer, who knew the plotters intimately, the original conception was that Stauffenberg should sacrifice himself, blowing himself up along with the Führer and such other top Nazis as he could catch at the Wolf's Lair. However, Stauffenberg was now convinced that he, rather than the aged Beck or the garrulous and passé Goerdeler, would arise as the new power in Germany, and so it was agreed that he would return to Berlin as soon as the task was accomplished.

The bomb was awaiting him when he arrived at the airport. General Helmuth Stieff, the hunchbacked 'poison dwarf', had prepared a neat little infernal device: a one-kilogramme bomb with a delayed-action fuse. A glass capsule held acid; once that was broken the acid dripped on to a wire which held the firing-pin taut; the thickness of the wire determined the time for the acid to eat through it and release the pin on to a percussion cap. Stieff had thoughtfully provided a pair of tongs so that the crippled Stauffenberg could more easily break the capsule, as he had only one hand and a mere three fingers on that. The package, neatly wrapped in a shirt, was transferred to Stauffenberg's brief-case.

Within minutes the special plane — provided on the orders of another member of the conspiracy, the man in charge of the

Home Army supplies, General Eduard Wagner — was airborne. The plane touched down at 10.15, and by 12.42 the briefcase was deposited under the table near Hitler's feet, The timetable to disaster had begun.

Eight minutes later it exploded, but it was established by the survivors in the room[1] that Hitler lived, with only minor injuries.

Stauffenberg and his aide von Haeften drove from the compound, having arranged transport with General Erïch Fellgiebel, chief of the communications branch at the Führer's HQ and *the man charged with the vital task of telephoning the conspirators in Berlin, who would then activate the Torgau men and take over the military communications of the Reich.*

Having seen the conference room explode in fire and smoke, Stauffenberg and Haeften concluded Hitler was dead, and they boarded their plane, which left immediately and arrived at Rangsdorf airfield some two hours later.

But as the British historian of the *Attentat*, Sir John Wheeler-Bennett, concludes: *no telephone call reached the conspirators in Berlin's Bendlerstrasse.* 'The failure of Fellgiebel to carry out his assignment as well as cutting Rastenburg off from Berlin and the rest of the Reich was as disastrous for the success of the revolt as the survival of Hitler.'

One telephone call stood between possible victory and certain defeat. Why did Fellgiebel not make it? Did he lose his nerve when he saw Hitler stagger, wounded but very much alive, from the bunker? But he knew that even if Hitler lived the conspiracy could still go ahead. Or was he swiftly seized because someone knew of his vital role in the conspiracy?[2] Did that same someone know also about the Torgau operation and betray the officer-prisoners there to the Nazis? Was that someone Colonel-General Heinz Guderian, Inspector General of Armoured Forces, who was in East Prussia at the time of the *Attentat*, who knew about the conspiracy (he was approached by no fewer than four of its leaders), who hours after the explosion was promoted to be Army Chief of Staff and who had concluded a secret compact with Nazi party chief Martin Bormann? The terrible 'maybes' accumulate.

Meanwhile in Berlin:

At dawn the principal actively employed conspirators — Gen-

---

[1]Four people were killed. Most of the remaining twenty-four were injured in varying degrees.

[2]General Fellgiebel was executed for treason on 4 September, 1944.

eral of Infantry, Friedrich Olbricht, his immediate staff and Berlin's commandant, Colonel-General von Hase, issued standby orders for Operation Valkyrie — the contingency plans to suppress internal trouble from whatever source — to the Reserve Army and training camps near Berlin. These officers awaited the arrival of older, more distinguished conspirators, at Bendlerstrasse HQ.

Yet, as Wheeler-Bennett observes:

> No provision had been made for wiring the headquarters for broadcasting, although it was essential that Beck (putative Head of State) and Witzleben (Shadow C-in-C of the Armed Services) should make their broadcasts to the German people and to the armed forces as soon as possible after the putsch . . . a feat which was surely not impossible with the co-operation of the Signal Corps.

The signal corps were waiting in Torgau. It is a measure of the success of the Bormann-Guderian Operation Secrecy that Torgau is not mentioned once in Wheeler-Bennett's mammoth volume.

In the afternoon the major military figures assembled awaiting the vital call from the Wolf's Lair. Among them was General Eric Hoepner and Field Marshal von Witzleben. Soon after three o'clock General Fritz Thiele — one of those who had been at Torgau three days previously — reported, 'Something is wrong. I have been in touch with Rastenburg [which, of course, Fellgiebel should have cut off]. The bomb has gone off but no one there seems to know who is alive or dead.' A little later Stauffenberg's aide Haefter phoned asking for a car to take them from Rangsdorf airport to the Bendlerstrasse. To a query about the Führer he answered brusquely 'He's dead.'

Von Hase as Commandant for Berlin received instructions 'Put Valkyrie into operation.' But at the same moment the time-serving head of the Reserve Army, General Fromm, whose signature all orders had to bear, put through a personal call to the Wolf's Lair to be told 'The Führer is safe. Where is your Chief of Staff, Colonel von Stauffenberg?'

When Stauffenberg arrived, Fromm told him 'You must shoot yourself.' And to Olbricht: 'Consider yourself under arrest.' Stauffenberg continued to assert that Hitler was dead and added, 'I saw his body carried out.' Olbricht then turned to Fromm and declared 'Herr General, it is *we* who are arresting *you*.'

Leaping from his chair, Fromm tried to grab his pistol but was overpowered. His arms were pinioned behind his back; he was disarmed and put under guard in an adjoining room.

Witzleben appointed his fellow-conspirator Hoepner to the command of the Home Army.

When SS Oberführer Piffräder arrived to arrest von Stauffen-berg — as discreetly as possible on the orders of Himmler — he was himself promptly arrested and put in the same room with Fromm, General von Kortzfleisch (the Nazi-minded commander of Military District III) and a number of their junior staff who remained loyal. They were rather like Captain Bligh and his companions who were permitted to live by the mutineers of the *Bounty*. The mutineers were to regret their clemency. So were the Berlin conspirators. At this point they thought they had won.

*   *   *

Back at Rastenburg . . .

At about three o'clock a freshly dressed Führer greeted the fallen Italian dictator, Benito Mussolini, who had chosen this extraordinary day to visit the HQ of his deliverer.

At half-past three Hitler ordered Himmler to crush the revolt, while at five o'clock Adolf and Benito took tea. The Nazi Chief-tains, hearing rumours of the attempt on the Führer's life rushed to the Wolf's Lair to declare their loyalty. Straightway they fell to quarrelling, Foreign Minister Ribbentrop and Grand Admiral Doenitz saying the Army had sold out to Britain; Ribbentrop yelling at Goering, 'I'm *von* Ribbentrop'; messages from units throughout Germany pouring into the Wolf's Lair asking, 'Are we to obey orders from the commander of the Home Army? What is happening?'

At six o'clock, after a day of confusion, protestation and recrimination, there was a telex message sent to all commands, including Bendlerstrasse: 'Obey orders signed only by Field Marshal Keitel or Reichsführer SS Heinrich Himmler. Adolf Hitler alive and well!'

Despite the telex order the conspirators decided to brazen things out. Declared Beck, 'We must go forward now whatever happens. Let us be firm. Let us be strong for Germany.' Stauf-fenberg, whether from desperation or conviction, answered query after query from generals throughout Europe:

All orders from the Home Army C-in-C are to be obeyed. Seize all wireless stations and information centres. Break all

SS opposition. Valkyrie is in full operation. Field Marshal von Witzleben and the Wehrmacht are in total control. You are to obey only orders from Witzleben and Hoepner.

Günther von Kluge, C-inC West, telephoned: 'Is Hitler dead or not? Am I to obey Keitel or Witzleben?' General Beck himself took this call. 'Will you place yourself under my command as Head of State?' Answer came there none. Kluge determined to sit on the fence until the iron entered his soul.

Half an hour later Berlin radio announced to the world that the Führer had been slightly hurt in a criminal attempt on his life, but would address the German people later in the evening.

From that moment on the conspiracy was finished.

And here is another incomprehensible blunder. Seizure of Berlin Radio should have been the first objective of the conspirators. Why did they fail to hold it? (Elements of the Home Army did take it for an hour or two and then quit.) Again the answer lies in Torgau. One hundred kilometres to the south were the officers who could have turned Berlin Radio into an instrument for the rebels instead of permitting it to become the weapon of their destruction.

For now there appeared on the scene the little limping doctor, Paul Josef Goebbels, the propaganda genius of the Third Reich, who had been informed of what had happened in the Wolf's Lair. He swiftly grasped the situation and unerringly sought out the one man who could, almost without firing a shot, end the generals' revolt. That man was Major Otto Ernst Remer.

Remer, a much decorated soldier and devout admirer of the Führer and National Socialism, should never have been entrusted with the task of mustering his guards battalion to surround the Government district. But the Panzer troops, who could have been expected to rally to the Wehrmacht, had been ordered to stay in their barracks *at the direct intervention of Heinz Guderian, telephoning from East Prussia.*

Through an intermediary — a Nazi officer named Hagen — Goebbels got in touch with Remer and the final bloody stages of the coup were launched.

At seven o'clock Goebbels, Nazi leader of Berlin as well as Minister of Propaganda and Popular Enlightenment, told Remer, 'The Führer lives. He will speak soon to the world. Meanwhile would you care to speak to him directly to reassure yourself that what I say is true?' Remer agreed. He knew Hitler's voice from personal experience, for he had received his Knight's Cross from the Führer's hands.

Adolf Hitler spoke on the telephone, and Remer was convinced. 'Place yourself and your unit under the direct orders of Reichsführer Himmler. He is the new head of the Home Army (the third in twelve hours!). Suppress all resistance with ruthless energy.'

Strangely, Remer and Goebbels had similar features, being fairly small and hollow-cheeked, with prominent cheek-bones, and excellent persuasive voices. These two[1] really settled the fate of the plot.

Field Marshal von Witzleben, in a kind of ghastly parody of Laurel and Hardy, remarked, 'This is a fine mess you've got me into'. He quit the Bendlerstrasse to return by car to his estate and soon after the biters were bit; officers of Fromm's staff overpowered their guards and pushed their way into the room occupied by the principal plotters. Olbricht's arms were grabbed before he could reach his pistol.

Stauffenberg dived for the door, and was shot in the back just as he reached the corridor.

Fromm formed a drumhead court-martial consisting of himself, and condemned the plotters to death.

The first detachments of Remer's troops entered the Bendlerstrasse, heard a shot and immediately released the safety catches of their rifles. But it was Colonel-General Ludwig Beck taking his own life.

Led by Lieutenant Schlee, the soldiers of Remer's countercoup occupied the whole building. Fromm proclaimed, 'In the name of the Führer a summary court-martial called by myself has reached the following verdict.' What he had already resolved was now to be implemented. Immediate execution of the plotters.

So Stauffenberg, bleeding profusely, his aide von Haeften, General Olbricht and a staff colonel Mertz von Quirnheim, were hustled into a courtyard below, and by the glare of Army truck headlights, were shot by firing squad.

Within half an hour another batch of conspirators were rounded up for rapid despatch, but suddenly a group of Gestapo

---

[1]Their destinies parted, however. Remer was promoted Major-General and after the war founded a Neo-Nazi Party, later dissolved. Goebbels and his wife committed suicide, and killed their six children, in the Führer's bunker hours before the Russians arrived.

chiefs arrived with orders from Reichsführer Himmler. No more summary executions. Every last suspect must be interrogated.

General Fromm was to pay dearly for this hitch in his liquidation time table. He himself was executed early in 1945 for his 'cowardly failure' to suppress the coup at the outset.

At midnight the Führer made a broadcast to assure his people that he lived, National Socialism lived, and the war would go on until victory was achieved.

Twenty hours had settled the fate of Germany.

Fourteen

'At the Touch of a Lever'?

And so a terrible vengeance supervened. The Führer vowed no one would escape, and in truth few did. Every one of the principals was either executed — many after suffering unspeakable tortures — or committed suicide.

A Court of Honour, on which sat Heinz Guderian, expelled the senior officers so that they could be tried by a people's court. In this way the Army was freed from the messy business of shooting its own and blotting its escutcheon. So Field Marshal von Witzleben and Generals von Hase, Stieff, Fellgiebel, and four junior officers stood shivering in shabby civilian clothing minus belts, braces, suspenders, collars, while the charade of a trial was presided over by the pitiless Nazi judge, Roland Freisler.

The 'trial' lasted a day. On 8 August all the accused were hanged from meat-hooks. 'Let them die like cattle,' screamed Hitler, who insisted that the gruesome ceremony be filmed. Thousands more followed these first victims, and the executions continued until Hitler's death nine months later. Under the *Sippeschaft* law (guilt by kinship) many more would have perished simply because they were related to the plotters. Fortunately, American troops reached wives and children before the SS killer gangs could complete the massacre begun on 20 July.

Could the coup have succeeded under any conceivable circumstances? It did. In Paris.

In the Hôtel Raphaël on the Avenue Kléber there existed a mirror image of the Bendlerstrasse in Berlin. Practically the entire staff of the Military Governor, Heinrich von Stuelpnagel, were active conspirators. In addition, General Hans Speidel, Rommel's Chief of Staff, liaised between the field command and the administrators. Von Hofacker maintained contact with Beck and Stauffenberg. Paris paid particular attention to keeping radio and telephone links to Berlin in first-class condition, so that when Operation Valkyrie was implemented no hitch would develop.

As well as being a military man, Stuelpnagel was a shrewd diplomat. He invited the leading Nazi Party man in Paris, Otto Abetz, to dine with him two days before the coup 'to size up the man who could call on the SS units in Paris'. Abetz, a cultured, witty, smooth character, was no last-ditcher. He had calculated the odds, and was well aware that the Allies would be in Paris within the month. He was ready — without in any way committing himself — to go along with any development which paved the way to peace in the West. Abetz would do nothing about a coup, but equally would do nothing to prevent it. Even the SS and the dreaded SD, the Sicherheitsdienst, in charge of internal security, lacked the crazed zeal of their fellows in the Fatherland and points east.

Paris was a cushy posting, much envied and railed against by those Germans in more battered and exposed parts of Fortress Europe. Fanaticism may well have mellowed in the soft allure of the City of Joy. Certainly the brooding menace of the Führer was 1,000 instead of 100 kilometres away, and the enemy — in the shape of the ever-advancing Anglo-American invaders — were practically friends compared with the Soviets and the Nazis.

Conditions were more favourable in Paris than in Berlin. But, allowing for the difference, Paris showed what could have happened if the men from Torgau had been employed as they were meant to be employed; cutting off the Führer's headquarters from contact with everyone; opening every avenue of communication to the plotters.

At 17.00 the longed-for message came over the telephone from Stauffenberg's cousin, Hofacker: 'Hitler is dead.' Then came Witzleben's first order: Crush the SS.

The Parisian conspiracy swung into action. The Wehrmacht soldiers in France hated the SS, who, through their cruelties and arrogance, brought down the retribution of the Resistance on the head of the ordinary *Feldgrau*. A spiral of violence operated thus: the SS would commit some revolting act and a German soldier would be murdered in revenge. The SS would collect some twenty or thirty hostages and shoot them if the guilty Frenchman was not handed over to the authorities; this in turn provoked

further attacks by the Resistance (who of course did not disting-
uish between the Wehrmacht and the SS), and so the murder and
counter-murder went on.

In the East the Waffen (armed) SS had earned a reputation for
courage against a brutal foe. There was a degree of camaraderie
between the Wehrmacht and the SS. In the West no such rapport
existed. And when the SS did move into combat they often used
the same inhuman tactics which had become routine in the sav-
age warfare in the east. Himmler's words on one SS Regiment,
Dirlewanger, provide reason enough for the Army's loathing:
'The tone of the regiment is, I may say, in many cases a medieval
one with cudgels and such things. If anyone expresses doubts
about winning the war he is likely to fall dead from the table.'[1]

The regiment was named after Oskar Dirlewanger, who had
been sentenced to two years' jail for offences against a minor in
1933. He was reported to have put on public display in Lublin in
Poland the death struggle of Jewish girls injected with strych-
nine.[2]

To honourable soldiers the SS represented a revolting departure from western Christian ethics. Moreover, many of the SS
were not German (the Dirlewanger Regiment had a number of
Frenchmen), and so it could be argued that foreigners were
helping to smear the German name.

All in all, the decent German soldier in the West had more
cause to hate the SS — and still more the SD, which spied on the
Wehrmacht — than the Allies. So when the 1st Motorized Rifle
Regiment was ordered to round up the SS and SD the soldiers
went about their task with a will. There was no resistance. The SS
headquarters in the Avenue Foch was seized; the SS commander
confined to the Hôtel Continental and his men imprisoned in the
Fort de l'Est. Paris was in the hands of the insurgents. At that
moment the war in the West could have been ended.

If Erwin Rommel had been in charge it surely would have been.
But three days had elapsed since his near-fatal wounding, and in
that period direct control of Army Group B had been taken by
Field Marshal Günther von Kluge.

There followed a bizarre dinner party at Kluge's headquarters

---

[1]Quoted in *S.S. Alibi of a Nation*, by Gerald Reitlinger.

[2]Evidence before International Military Tribunal, Nuremberg. No testimony was
given by Dirlewanger, however: he escaped at the war's end.

at La Roche-Guyon. Stuelpnagel, Hofacker and Speidel were invited.[1] The black-out was relaxed a fraction to allow candles to flicker through the open windows, opened to ease the sultry atmosphere.

Hitler lived: on that point there was unanimous agreement. But what to do here in the West far from the malign influence of the Wolf's Lair in distant East Prussia? Stuelpnagel was adamant: 'It is still possible to take independent action. You, Field Marshal, have pledged yourself to act; your word and honour are at stake. Something must be done.' Von Kluge rose to his feet; 'Gentlemen, nothing can be done. The Führer lives. Now let us go in to dinner.'

Hopelessly torn between dread of a vengeful Führer and the certainty that hundreds of thousands of German soldiers would die unless he acted to bring the war in the West to an end, 'clever Kluge' went into dinner. The opportunity was lost. The man who could have changed the course of the war lay unconscious in hospital. The man who sat at the head of an elegant dinner table sipping wine did not have in him the stuff of hero, or martyr, or even traitor.

Stuelpnagel tried one last gambler's throw. Taking Kluge by the arm, he murmured, 'Action has already been taken against the SS.' Quickly Kluge calculated: 'I gave no such orders. If I were you I would change into civilian clothes and go into hiding.'

No one did any such thing. The generals, whether those involved in the coup or the temporizers playing both sides against the middle, demonstrated a remarkable indifference to their safety. Any one of them at that dinner party could have vanished — to turn up shortly afterwards in the Allied camp. Junior officers on the fringe of the conspiracy, such as von Herwarth, discussed the possibility of deserting only to dismiss it as unworthy. Honour of the Officer Corps was still their most precious commodity, however tarnished by obedience to Nazism. The prisoners at Torgau would have understood.

The conspirators returned from La Roche-Guyon to Paris and their doom. Over the radio — that radio which should have been in the hands of Torgau's communication experts — the raucous voice of Robert Ley, the podgy, semi-literate chief of the Nazi

---

[1]As recounted in Wheeler-Bennett's *Nemesis of Power,* using the recorded evidence of Speidel and those survivors to whom Stuelpnagel spoke on his return to Paris.

Labour front (the epitome of all that aristocratic generals loathed) gloatingly previewed the Führer's address.

'If only we'd had a little more revolutionary blood in our veins', lamented one of the plotters. Alas, men trained in the hierarchical tradition — authority downward, responsibility upward — do not make effective rebels. Paris, which had fallen without a blow, was now surrendered by the victors to the vanquished: the SS were released in a dawn handover at the Hotel Raphaël after the death's-head Scharführers, Standatenführers and all the other little 'führers' had been assured, again and again, that they would not fall victim to their own ploy by stepping out of their cells to an illusory freedom — i.e., shot while trying to escape.

As neither side wanted to give the French Resistance the satisfaction of witnessing internecine strife, a story was concocted that Operation Valkyrie was an exercise to test internal security! Indeed, that was not too far from the truth as originally envisaged as camouflage for the plotters.

As the sun of 21 July rose in the Parisian sky nemesis approached. The telephone rang in Stuelpnagel's tastefully furnished office. It was Berlin. He was to report immediately to the Reich capital. Stuelpnagel chose to go by car, and near the First World War battlefield of Verdun he shot himself. The greater tragedy, however, was that he did not die; he was blinded but lived to be interrogated by the Gestapo. Both he and Hofacker probably implicated Rommel: the first under the influence of anaesthetics, the second as a result of torture.

No sooner had Rommel recovered from his wounds and started to recuperate at his home near Ulm than the Führer struck once more. Two officers called at the Rommel household and told his wife and son that they would like to brief the Field Marshal on his next assignment. In fact they carried with them a letter from Hitler's henchman, Wilhelm Keitel, outlining the charges of complicity which had been extracted from Hofacker. Rommel had a choice: go to Berlin and attempt to answer these charges or commit suicide (which would be officially announced as 'death from the effect of his wounds') and ensure a great State funeral for himself and the safety of his family, plus a Field Marshal's pension for them. Rommel chose the latter. On 14 October he took poison. On the 17th he received his State funeral. It was his last posthumous service to Führer and Fatherland.

For if Erwin Rommel had faced his accusers the Third Reich

could hardly have survived. Rommel was almost as popular as Hitler: he could have provoked a crisis of confidence sufficient to undermine mortally the fighting morale of the armed forces.

As soon as order had been restored in Paris, Rommel's titular chief, von Kluge, was at pains to try to restore that morale, pledging his own and his soldiers, undying loyalty to Adolf Hitler. He might have saved himself the bother. First Heinz Guderian, then Hofacker (under torture) gave away his double game. On 15 August 1944, the deadly summons to Berlin reached Clever Kluge. He penned his last dispatch to the Wolf's Lair.

> My Führer, [he wrote] I have always admired your greatness, your conduct in the gigantic struggle and your iron will to maintain yourself and National Socialism. If fate is stronger than your will and genius, so is Providence. You have fought an honourable and great fight. History will prove that for you. Show yourself now great enough to put an end to a hopeless struggle. I depart from you, my Führer, in the consciousness that I did my duty to the utmost.

As with Stuelpnagel, von Kluge set off by car for First World War battlefields and swallowed poison somewhere near Metz. He was dead on arrival at hospital.

So ended the conspiracy in the West.

As for the five men who had presented themselves at Torgau, they each met a grisly fate. The capture of the conspirators of the Bendlerstrasse swiftly yielded the information which the Gestapo had failed to uncover in routine surveillance. Spurred on by Heinrich Himmler and Ernst Kaltenbrunner, the scar-faced giant who headed Reich Security, the interrogators were able to cast their net wide.

Into it went the suave orator, Caesar von Hofacker, who had so inspired the prisoners. After being vilely tortured he was executed five days before Christmas 1944.

Captain Count Ulrich Wilhelm von Schwerin-Schwanenfeld, friend of Die Wasserkante, answered back in court, denouncing his accusers. He was hanged on 8 September 1944.

Dr Carl Sack, the jurist, almost survived. He was murdered in Flossenberg concentration camp only days before it was liberated in April 1945. Sack was one of the earliest anti-Nazi conspirators. As far back as 1938 he had offered to prosecute a captive Hitler before a panel of psychiatrists who were confidently expected to pronounce the Führer insane and confine him to a lunatic asylum.

General Fritz Thiele was hanged on 15 September, 1944, and Colonel-General von Thüngen followed him to the grave six weeks later.

They perished with courage and honour. Whatever failings they had, it required a high degree of valour to conspire against a totalitarian state. True, they lacked revolutionary ardour and cold-bloodedness (for example, they should never have permitted Fromm and his staff to survive), but their prime error, and that of the rest of the conspirators, was an elementary blunder for professional soldiers: failure to secure communications.

Everything comes back to Torgau. Had these 1,200 experts been transported the 100 kilometres to Berlin, and had General Fellgiebel at the Wolf's Lair carried out his orders to cut the lines from the Führer's headquarters, would the putsch of 20 July have succeeded?

If what happened in Paris is any guide — yes. A comparatively small number of non-political soldiers, resolutely led, could have disarmed the SS in scores of cities. The inmates of military prisons similar to Torgau could have supplied additional expert and trusted personnel.

So long as the Führer's headquarters could not pour out counter-orders, the military would have obeyed instructions from such venerated figures as von Witzleben — the first man to be given a Field Marshal's baton by Hitler. Some others — Goerdeler, Hoepner and Co.— might not have inspired similar respect, for they had been dismissed by the regime. But Witzleben had retired with honour. What more natural than that he, in the absence of the Führer, and in the face of some apparent SS skulduggery, should assume command of the armed forces of the Reich?

If von Witzleben had been able to broadcast to the Reich, and occupied Europe, on the evening of 20 July he could have got away with practically anything.

According to *Signal*, the magazine of the Wehrmacht, Dr Goebbels's office at 8-9 Wilhelmplatz, Berlin, would have been the communicator's delight. 'The touch of a lever suffices and with the aid of up-to-date technical installations Dr Goebbels can immediately switch off any programmes of the broadcasting stations in greater Germany and himself speak through the microphone to all listeners.'

'At the touch of a lever' would have been one of the jobs for the Torgau brigade. The job that was never accomplished. And for the want of a touch the battle was lost.

With the help of Torgau technicians, the Third Reich would have been in the hands of those who controlled its central nervous system: the main broadcasting stations. Whoever 'blew the whistle' on Torgau, and prevented the 1,200 experts from taking up their positions on the morning of 20 July, effectively destroyed the coup. No one can be certain, but the evidence points clearly to the genial buccaneer of armoured warfare, the man who broke the French at Abbeville, the second most popular soldier after Rommel in the Reich — smiling Heinz Guderian. That certainly was the view of General Niedermayer, who, by remaining aloof from the conspiracy while enjoying close and comradely relations with fellow-officers whom he had known for thirty years, was ideally placed to measure the action and reaction of those who played leading parts in the high drama.

Niedermayer, of course, committed nothing to paper; he simply passed on his views verbally when he himself became a prisoner in Torgau — for 'defeatist talk', remarking to his staff that he thought the war was lost.

Guderian naturally said nothing of such matters in his post-war writings. But the circumstantial case against him is powerful. One of the junior plotters, Hans von Herwarth, went to sound him out some time before 20 July. Herwarth reported[1]:

> He was obviously a decent person, who knew full well the war was lost. He was popular with his soldiers. He was held to be a kind of saint among the armoured troops, and could have been immensely effective in rallying them to the cause of the Resistance. Instead he chose duty to the bitter end, even assuming a new assignment after having first been briefly demoted. *One can only wonder why he accepted this from Hitler, of whom he was so openly critical.*

The more Guderian played along with the conspirators — agreeing with them about the awfulness of the Nazis and their own gloomy assessment of the progress of the war — the more he would learn of their plans. He admitted in his memoirs that he

---

[1]*Against Two Evils,* by Hans von Herwarth.

learned on 18 July of moves to make peace in the West, and this may have alerted him to the imminence of the Berlin coup, about the preparations for which he was already well informed. He then arranged to be out of Berlin on the fateful day 20 July, and confined his armoured troops to barracks. In this way he freed himself from pressure from the conspirators — who were old cronies — while continuing to exercise control over his Panzer units by telephone from East Prussia; a vital location, within easy reach of the Führer's headquarters. He was able during the vital hours to ban the movement of the armoured troops who might — given their antagonism to the SS —have been used by the conspirators.

But all the careful positioning and balancing depended on excellent, uninterrupted communications — hence the need to neutralize the Torgau factor in Operation Valkyrie. The way to do that was to prevent two officers ever getting to Festung Zinna in the early hours of 20 July to lead the convoy (where trucks were already in position) from Torgau into Berlin.

Whether these officers were quietly picked up by the civil or military police or the SD will never be known. It is unlikely to be the result of an oversight on the part of the plotters, considering the lengths to which they had gone to gather so many dissident experts in one place, and to send five of the principal participants to give them their orders, seventy-two hours before the putsch.

No, the probability is that there was some tip-off — perhaps to German Military Intelligence, which had been communications-orientated since the uncovering of the Russian spy-rings, and was alert to the overwhelming importance of radio telecommunications. There was no reason for Guderian to have done this himself; the warning about Torgau could have been passed through a number of channels to allow him to avoid any personal involvement.

Once Torgau had been eliminated Guderian would clearly want its existence and potential expunged from the records — to keep his own reputation clean with the Wehrmacht, and to spare the German Army yet another dreadful example of treason.

Guderian's appointment to Army Chief of Staff (on 21 July!); his agreement with the Nazi Party chief Martin Bormann to clear the Wehrmacht from the taint of betraying their oath to the Führer; his general order blaming a few 'cowardly officers'; his readiness to judge the conspirators and to expel them from the Army into the merciless clutches of the people's court; and his defence of the Hitler salute for the Army are all of a pattern.

Heinz Guderian may not have betrayed the conspiracy against Hitler, but it is almost certain that he betrayed the key element which would have allowed the conspiracy to triumph — Torgau.

Fifteen

Nemesis

In the early hours of 20 July, the day that was to see the dawn of a new and better Germany, I, Jakob Kersten, awoke with the feeling that something was terribly wrong. There was a stillness about the Festung I could not understand. At first light weren't we supposed to see the trucks line up in the Festung yard to speed our happy warriors to their rendezvous with destiny in Berlin? Shouldn't the corridors be full of the sound of happy men, walking out of a nightmare and preparing for the action they craved? Yet everything was deathly quiet.

I slipped into my wooden clogs (no one had promised me a 'return to honour'. I still had to wear the clogs of shame, branding me as an escapee), climbed the boiler-house steps and entered the fortress corridors.

My fears were confirmed. The corridors of Torgau were deserted; not a single guard was in sight, but instead of this being a sign that everyone was liberated, the opposite was the case. The cell doors were all firmly locked. I walked from one to another, overcome with a mounting sense of doom. The questions crowded in: Where were the guards who had been posted to us a week before, to ensure freedom of the inmates? Where were the two officers whom von Hofacker had said would bring final instructions from Berlin? Why were the cell doors locked, and who had locked them? What was happening?

The same questions now penetrated into the stone compartments. As morning light infiltrated the prison men started pounding on their locked doors. The sound grew louder, echoing through the deserted corridors, reverberating from the lofty walls.

Prisoners began to call out. At first their tone was angry, authoritative and demanding: 'Guard, open this bloody door! What the hell is going on?'

But then, when there was no answer, anger gave way to fear, frustration and despair. The officers who had sung *Deutschland über alles* with such hope and confidence now began to suspect a terrible turn of events. They kicked and screamed and wept. Some charged the doors with their shoulders as though they imagined they could break down the steel enclosures as once their tanks had demolished all in their path.

These proud fellows, so full of elation a few hours before, were in the grip of fear made sharper and more pervasive by ignorance of what was happening. Suddenly I realized I was one of the handful of people who could look outside and find out.

I returned to my boiler-house retreat, carefully closing the door, and lifted myself up by way of a coal-stack to peer out of the window.

There were guards at the main gate all right, but they were the old guards, the ones who had tyrannized over us. Of the new guards, the conspirators' guards, there was not a sign. They had vanished as swiftly and inexplicably as they had appeared. With surgical precision guards had been exchanged, all doors locked and Torgau as effectively cut off from the outside world as Torgau's inmates had planned to cut off the Wolf's Lair.

Yet things were not quite as they had been before. Reinforcing the old guards, who were grouped near the entrance, stood military police armed with pistols and rifles. A machine-gun was rigged, ready for us — and its muzzle was trained on the centre of the prison block.

Climbing down from my perch, heart fluttering, stomach churning, I got out the crystal set I'd assembled. Feverishly I fiddled with it until Berlin Radio came through clearly. Hour after hour, oblivious to the need for food, ignoring nature's calls for fear of missing anything, I waited for the broadcast Hofacker had promised us. Nothing in the morning. Nothing in the afternoon: except the war communiqués, music, sentimental and martial, hints on how to cook tasty meals with ersatz victuals. Nothing . . . until the announcement that a criminal attempt had been made on the life of the Führer, that it had failed and that Adolf Hitler would address the world.

I sat staring at the set. If I felt demoralized, what must the poor devils in the cells be feeling? They wouldn't know as yet about the failure of the coup, but they must guess that things had gone totally awry. When I heard Hitler pouring out his hatred on the ether I could think only that this was the voice of death for the prisoners of Torgau.

Had I been a supporter of the generals' putsch I would have gone from cell to cell telling them the bad news, preparing them, mentally at least, for the terrors to come. But I didn't care for the generals. To me, to Die Wasserkante, they were marginally better than the Nazis, but we did not share the pro-West, anti-Russian policy of most of them. Why should I care what happened to colonels and majors and captains upstairs? Yet I did. I could feel ice in my bowels at the brutish vengeance which would descend on them.

And what of me? Would I be left as witness to desolation? I resolved to remain in the boiler-house, where I had my own small store of provisions, to keep my head down and hope for the best.

Next day, 21 July, passed in eerie, unbelievable silence. The old guards, the military police, the machine-gun, remained in position. I went up once to the corridors, where an uncanny quietness reigned, broken occasionally by the odd cry and outburst of weeping. I assumed the prisoners were not being fed. They had water and toilets in their cells.

22 July followed the same pattern. But then, in the early evening, Hauptmann Friedrich appeared. I had not seen him for two or three weeks — since Torgau was virtually taken over by the conspirators — and what a change had been wrought! He looked a positive wreck. His face was drawn, there were huge shadows under his eyes which suggested he had not slept for days, and his breath smelt strongly of schnapps. Our roles were reversed. He was the suppliant. I was . . . well, not the master, but at least, in my own kingdom, the host. I offered him some acorn coffee. He accepted gratefully, and together we sipped the strong black brew.

Friedrich stared vacantly ahead. I wondered: had he been in the plot and was waiting for the inevitable retribution? Or had he betrayed the plotters and regretted his action? Were these anguished features a sign of remorse?

What a contrast there was between this deflated figure and the stern, bombastic, masterful Hauptmann Friedrich of former days, who had such a passion for drill and Prussian discipline. Today he was a weak, ailing, pitiful creature. I could feel sorry for him, as I no longer feared the rigid rule of Torgau: 'Never speak until you are spoken to.'

Tapping Friedrich gently on the knee to rouse him from his melancholy reverie, I asked, 'Are you in danger?'

'No. I have had nothing to do with the events of the last few weeks and have been under surveillance myself; unable to move from my office, forbidden to give orders. No, I do not think the SS will be after me. But those others' — he pointed upstairs and shook his head mournfully. 'They have been horribly betrayed.'

'By whom?'

'I honestly have no idea. I truly am just a soldier who obeys orders. When I am ordered to do or not to do something by a senior officer, I concur.' I wondered if this would be his excuse when the SS began their investigations.

As I was to discover later, no fewer than four hundred special investigators had been recruited by Gruppenführer 'Gestapo' Müller, and they were working round the clock to establish the full ramifications of the plot. The delay in dealing with Torgau had a simple technical explanation — it was not yet our turn.

'They have no chance of survival,' muttered Friedrich, still contemplating the fate of the prisoners. 'Nor has Germany,' he added surprisingly. 'We are doomed. The Army leaders have lost all honour. The Party fanatics will fight to the last cartridge. What has Hitler said? Not to the eleventh hour, but till five past midnight. No surrender. No repeat of 1918. So Germany will be destroyed. There will be nothing left. You know my own house has been wiped out?'

'Yes, but your family is safe. Possessions can always be found again.'

He would not be comforted. Strangely, I found sadness for him within myself. Everything this man believed in — country, Army, Party, Führer — was disintegrating. I ought to have been exultant. I wasn't.

I tried a little philosophy: 'Every end has a new beginning.'

'No, I have seen two world wars and one new beginning. If your new beginning is anything like the last one I don't want to know.' Maybe that exchange was an indication of the democratic Germany to come.

He levered himself out of his seat and made towards the steps. Half-way up he paused and turned: 'Come what may, you must stay down in the boiler-house tomorrow. To go out into the Festung would prove fatal.' He raised his hand in salutation, reached the landing and carefully locked the door behind him.

Left alone, I puzzled and wondered. Who? Who had betrayed the secret of Torgau? If Hauptmann Friedrich was in the clear, then who else would have sold out the plotters? Von Hofacker?[1] Who was the Judas? Was he here or outside? The questions kept repeating themselves in my mind, and I stayed awake until the early hours.

I had just fallen into a fitful doze when a frightful noise jerked me awake. I sat up, clearing my mind of sleep, and focused on the din upstairs. There was a roaring sound of commands, of cell doors being thrown open, of marching footsteps ringing out in the corridors and on the cobblestones of the Festung yard. I clambered on to my stack of coal bricks and peered out of the window. What I saw made me catch my breath. Involuntarily I ducked down lest I be seen, for there in the Festung yard stood men from the SS Dirlewanger unit — the executioners.

No one who has not experienced the dread which an élite body of killers inspires can appreciate the terror that means. I believe I moaned, as though I were already in their grasp. Each SS man gripped a machine pistol, and in the roof of the administrative building two machine-gun posts commanded the entire square.

On the east side of the Festung yard, its rear facing towards the main prison building, stood an open-backed Army truck. Standing on the tailboard were two SS officers surveying the scene with cold, malevolent stares.

From the main prison block, hundreds of Torgau prisoners were marching out in military formation. I guessed about four hundred. They marched with precision, in step, arms swinging; tradition did not waver. But then a harsh voice cracked out and these so-proper officers broke into a trot. They had been ordered to move 'at the double', just like a bunch of rookies.

Gradually they sorted themselves out in ranks, each man one arm's length from the one in front and one arm's length from the one at his side. The voice (I could not make out its source) barked out once more, ordering the officers to stand at attention and keep quiet.

An ominous silence fell on the parade ground. Someone

[1]He was tortured, but not until well after the events described here had taken place.

coughed, and was swiftly hushed. Then the more senior SS officer, a Hauptsturmführer, began to speak.

'The authorities have been made aware of the happenings in Torgau. They are aware of the Festung's involvement in the planned putsch against the Führer. The putsch has failed.' Here not even the legendary discipline of the German officer corps could prevent a collective sigh, a sort of mass whimper. The SS officer paused and resumed in a louder, more snarling tone. 'The Führer is alive and well, and has demanded that the traitors responsible be brought to justice.

'This affair has brought a humiliating shame on the Armed Forces of Germany. The full extent of that shame cannot and will not be allowed to reach the outside world. The SS will make sure of that.

'Already many of those responsible for the planning of the putsch have been arrested and shot by their own loyal colleagues.[1] It is the opinion of many of us that you, men of Torgau, who willingly offered yourselves as tools to be used in the destruction of the Führer, should be shot.

'However the Führer, in his infinite mercy, has decreed that you be given a chance to redeem yourselves by dying for the Fatherland. The Führer has decreed that you be allowed to shed your blood fighting alongside regiments such as the Dirlewanger on the Eastern Front. Those who wish to avail themselves of this glorious opportunity should break ranks and re-form on the right-hand side of the square.'

Men rushed to the right, some almost falling over in their haste to do the bidding of the SS whom, only three days before, they had vowed to exterminate like rats. Three days ago they were ready for the march on Berlin. Now they scuttled to form ranks for what even the most bone-headed must have known was a death march; a mere postponement of the inevitable. For the 'special battalions' were scheduled for massacre on the field of honour. And that was the reason those brave officers were hastening to obey the decree of their executioners: honour, the shroud without which no German officer's career was complete.

The manoeuvre over, a major — the one who had led the singing of *Deutschland über alles* after Hofacker's oration and who, I'd heard, was listed to play an important role in Operation

---

[1] At that time General Fromm, who had ordered the executions, was still apparently regarded — publicly anyway — as a loyalist.

Valkyrie — detached himself from the assembled ranks and approached the Army truck at the double. He skidded to a halt and, standing rigidly to attention, intoned, 'Report the company present and correct.'

Like lightning the SS officer responded — by raising his boot and kicking the major full in the face.

'I am not interested in reports from traitors. For that dishonourable insubordination you will be shot.' The death sentence seemed to have no effect on the major. He stood stock-still, a pillar of military rectitude. The blood flowed from his mouth and nose, staining the uniform of which he had once been so proud. Then the SS officer turned away as though the 'former major' had ceased to exist — which would very soon be the case.

He focused his attention on the area of the square where the volunteers had assembled. Then he noticed that five prisoners had remained in their original positions and were now gathering together. He leapt down from the tailboard and strode across to them. He stood about two metres from them, eyes blazing in a fury, and said, 'Did you hear me correctly?' No answer.

'Did you hear me?' he screamed. This time one of the officers stepped forward a pace. 'Yes, we heard.' Amazingly the SS officer gave him and his fellows a second chance.

'Will you serve the Fürher?' The same man spoke again: 'No, we will serve only Germany, the true Germany.' He drew himself up to his full height: he must have been nearly two metres tall. The two men stared at one another, and an age seemed to pass. Then the SS officer's eyes wavered and he took a step back.

'You understand what your action means?'

'Of course.'

'Very well then,' said the SS man, nodding his head ever so briefly in a sign of respect. 'You will be shot at first light tomorrow.' He clicked his heels, about-turned and marched back to the truck. On his way he flicked a hand towards two of his troopers who, machine pistols in hand, corralled the five dissidents and hustled them towards the death cells.

Petrified, I continued to look into the yard through my broken window-pane. I wanted to tear myself away from this scene of domestic tragedy — Germans killing Germans, each sure that they were the true patriots. As if there weren't enough Germans being killed on the battlefields of Europe — east, west and south!

With the five traitors (or heroes) safely under lock and key the

390 or so were marched off to the railway station.

Another batch of 400 then marched on to the square and the process was repeated. As it was once more with the final 400. By now all 1,200 of the special prisoners at Festung Zinna had been processed. From that total seven more prisoners had elected to join the five consigned to the death cells. The rest had chosen to die on the Eastern Front for something they didn't believe in. Inevitably it would be the Eastern Front, for as they would be wearing special penal identification and associated with the SS, they would die at the hands of the Russians if captured, whereas they would be spared by the Anglo-Americans in the West or in Italy. Surrender was therefore not an option open to them. Not that these brave, disciplined Germans would surrender to the Soviets even if their lives were to be spared. Keeping German soil free from Asiatic Bolshevism was a holy duty. They would discharge it to the bitter end.

With the main business of the morning concluded, SS Dirlewanger prepared to depart. But before they pulled out there was the matter of the insubordinate former major.

Still he stood there to attention, stiff as a waxwork, the blood congealed on his uniform, lips shredded where the jack-boot's heel had caught him, nose swollen and red as a clown's.

Two of the Dirlewanger approached. One stood in front of the prisoner, the other behind him. They ordered him to kneel. The SS man facing the major kicked him smartly in the groin and he sprawled to the ground; the other SS man coolly put his pistol to the major's neck and fired. The Dirlewangers walked away. I saw their expressions. They looked pleased with themselves, as though they had shot a rabid dog which could have spread infection.

So the 1,200 — less 13 — prisoners left Festung Zinna to unknown deaths on the 1,500-kilometre Russian front. They might have changed history. Instead they fertilized the plains of Eastern Europe, and with their passing Festung Zinna's role in the anti-Hitler plot was virtually erased.

With the Dirlewanger gone, I came down from my perch, and took stock of the situation. What of the 'old guard' members whom I had seen the previous day at the main gate? Would they return to duty? What of Hauptmann Friedrich? What above all of myself, the clog-clogging Dutchman? Would I remain part of the furniture or be spotted — and eliminated?

Answers to some of my questions arrived in the welcome appearance of Ernst, one of the very few decent members of the old guard, carrying a kettleful of soup and a loaf of bread. Hauptmann Friedrich also passed through on his way to the shower room after making sure the central-heating system was operating satisfactorily.

Ernst explained that the Dirlewanger had initially confined the old guard to their quarters — which was where they had been sent when the anti-Hitler front-line troops had arrived at Torgau.

'What happened to them — to the front-line fellows?' I asked.

'They were collected by the SS in the early hours of 20 July, herded into trucks and taken to God knows where. Some of them were badly beaten.'

'So what happens now?'

'Good lord, it's only just begun. The SS are in control throughout Germany. We are not allowed to give the Army salute any more. We are required to give the Nazi salute and shout 'Heil Hitler.'[1]

'What's more', he went on, 'Himmler is in supreme command of the Home Forces. The Army thought it was taking over. Instead it's the ruddy SS. God, I wish the bloody war was over.'

Then he looked round fearfully lest someone should be listening. That was the automatic reaction in the Third Reich to seditious talk.

Hauptmann Friedrich returned, spruce and shining after his shower and obviously ready to collaborate with the new order; probably thankful that for the moment he was not being held responsible for the manner in which high-up plotters had used Torgau for their own ends. He told me to resume my normal duties.

Five-thirty was my normal waking hour, but on this day I roused myself much earlier and set about the usual routine; going to the kitchen to prepare ersatz coffee for the guards in return for real coffee for myself. The Feldwebel in charge of catering was an understanding soul who enjoyed his rest.

Duty done, I woke the Feldwebel and, armed with a billican of fresh-brewed coffee, I made tracks for the main prison building

---

[1] This was the so-called Goering request. The Reichsmarschall asked for the Hitler salute to be introduced into the Wehrmacht. The Führer graciously consented. The Wehrmacht returned to the traditional salute on the orders of Hitler's successor, Admiral Doenitz, six days before Germany's surrender.

and the comfort of my boiler billet.

Suddenly the tranquillity was shattered by the closing of all doors and the bellowing of commands. It was a repeat performance of the Dirlewanger's arrival. When I arrived at the main building the guard on the main door warned me to take care — the SS had returned. The poor fellow was so agitated he couldn't swallow a mouthful of my real coffee.

To reach the entrance to the boiler-house I had to pass through the central, circular area of the Festung where the four wings conjoined. I found the guard there in a worse state of funk than his mate at the main gate.

'Here, Dutchman,' he muttered, 'a special commando of the SS have come to execute those twelve rebels, so behave yourself.'

'Bloody hell, I'd better make myself scarce.' I had just reached the door giving access to the boiler-room and safety when I was overcome by curiosity. I wanted to see if the SS were from the Dirlewanger or another division. So instead of going to my haven I sneaked a glance into the west wing where the condemned men lay and glimpsed a squad of SS men under the command of a Sturmbannführer. On the cuff of each man's sleeve was a black band, and embroidered in silver the two words 'Das Reich', denoting one of the most feared divisions in Germany.[1] I had seen quite enough and was about to beat a swift retreat to the boiler-house, but just as I reached the topmost step a curt command brought me to an abrupt halt. I shall never forget the voice as long as I live.

'Prisoner, come here.'

The words weren't spoken so much as hissed. They had to be directed at me, because I was the only prisoner outside his cell. I put down my billican, realizing I had committed a blunder which could well cost me my life, and retraced my steps.

'Prisoner, report yourself.' The Sturmbannführer was standing six metres away on the other side of the steel bars which secured the west wing. I reported myself in the appropriate fashion, stressing the words 'commandeered for central-heating duty', hoping that would suffice to explain my presence outside the boiler-room door. There was a moment's silence. The cold eyes looked me up and down.

[1]The division was in action in France at this period (they had been involved in the Oradour-sur-Glane massacre a few weeks before) but security detachments were on home service for counter-coup measures.

Then the Sturmbannführer motioned me to come to him. The guard rushed to open up and I found myself once more in death row. I had not the slightest doubt that I was being placed on execution duty: the gruesome business of preparing the condemned for death and carting away their bullet-ridden corpses.

My stomach heaved at the memory and I had difficulty in breathing as I recalled the fetters around my ankles which had reduced me to the level of a chained animal. And after I had witnessed the executions would I be executed myself? That was standard SS practice: to eliminate those who had seen too much.

Why in God's name had I wanted to see which set of SS men would carry out this particular liquidation? It was extraordinary how brainwashed I'd become, reading the German press and listening to the radio, before I had been sent to Torgau. Every bulletin from the front would illustrate in fine detail the exploits of the Waffen SS divisions: Adolf Hitler or Totenkopf or Das Reich or Viking, or any one of a dozen more. Against all my inclinations I wanted to see these supermen whom the Nazis continually likened to the Spartans; who had their own code of honour enshrined in the rules of the *Brüderschaft* and their own ferocious discipline — up to two years of harsh imprisonment for being two days absent without leave.

If the SS had been merely mercenary killers I would not have felt this icy dread; nor would I ever have risked stealing a glance at them. This was their terrible fascination, and I was paying a high price for yielding to it.

I stood rigidly awaiting my orders. In due course the twelve condemned were brought out of their cells. Did they, minutes from eternity, contemplate their fate — without trial, without publicity, without recourse to any appeal? Probably not. They knew the score. I had no means of discovering whether or not they had been permitted to relay last messages to their loved ones.

They were naked. Each man carried his set of fetters and manacles from which he had recently been released. They were ordered to drop their chains and fall into line. I was given a bundle of green paper costumes, the death dresses; I passed out one to each prisoner, walking slowly to give a little pitiful dignity to the grisly, squalid occasion.

I recognized the last in line. He was the one who had spoken up for the original five, the one who had defied the Hauptsturmführer of the SS Dirlewanger. I longed to embrace this man; to grasp his hand in tribute to outstanding valour. In doing that, of course, I would have joined the death line. Even so, it was difficult to hide my feelings. I managed a faint smile, trying to convey something of what was in my mind — courage, comrade, you are almost there; soon you will be free of all this. I think he understood me. He inclined his head a fraction.

The twelve now had to wait for the order to proceed to the place of execution and then wait again for the sun to rise. I knew what to expect; they didn't — poor bastards.

So they stood there silent on the square with no one, no chaplain, no priest to help them through the last moments of life. Some did not move a muscle, staring into the muzzles of the rifles now raised by the firing squad, while others had difficulty in controlling their limbs. They trembled from head to toe, desperate to retain the last shreds of manhood, fighting their last battle against fear. One or two looked as if they had already departed this world. Their eyes were glazed, their expression placid, matter-of-fact.

All of them gazed at the billowing clouds, reddening with the rising sun. Now most of them began to whisper to themselves. Were they saying goodbye to this world or praying for the next? Asking for strength and courage? God alone had the answer. He was nearer to them than I was.

There was a sharp intake of breath as the Sturmbannführer raised his arm and cried, 'Take aim.' The condemned jerked their bodies stiff as though attempting to resist the entrance of the bullets. They tilted their heads backward and lifted their eyes to the sky. They took their last look at the sun — as raw and red as blood . . .

The twelve lay sprawled on the ground, their blood mixing with the sandy soil and generating a fine pink haze as it met the morning air.

The volley had been accurate, as one would have expected from experienced executioners. Each victim had a large red hole through the left side of his chest. Their hearts were shredded.

I checked that no spark of life remained, straightened their twisted limbs and wiped my hands clean on their paper costumes. I closed sightless eyes and noted that a number wore positively happy expressions. It was the happiness of peace.

In contrast the faces of their killers bore the mark of lust. They stared intently at the dead; lips curled back, their tongues flicking from their mouths. They were deeply flushed and breathing heavily — as though they had derived something akin to sexual pleasure from what they had done.

Turning back to the dead — with relief — I lifted them, one by one, into the cart and wheeled them away to the area set aside for their mass burial. As I did so my back cracked in fear as I expected the sound of a bullet to end my part in the performance. Minutes passed. I carried on with my sombre task, and then — the square was empty. The SS detachment had marched off. For the moment at least I had been spared.

It has always been accepted that the first four victims of Hitler's revenge killings were the officers executed in Berlin on the evening of 20 July. But those who died in Berlin were shot on the orders of General Fromm to protect himself. They were scapegoats. When Kaltenbrunner and Skorzeny arrived at the Bendlerstrasse they immediately prevented further executions on the orders of their chief, Reichsführer Himmler, so as to preserve the conspirators for interrogation. The first victims of official vengeance were the twelve officers shot at Torgau.

They symbolized that strange dichotomy between chivalry and unblinking obedience which characterized the German officer class. But for their courage and sense of honour there can be only unstinting admiration.

Sixteen

'Like the French Revolution'

In the weeks following the unsuccessful putsch a strange, brooding silence enveloped Torgau. It wasn't that the prison remained empty for long — ordinary military prisoners, unconnected with the putsch, started filling the north and west wings again, and even 'normal' executions resumed — but the atmosphere was altered, from one of frenetic activity to a kind of dead tranquillity. The east wing, where the coup had been prepared, was completely empty.

Then early in August a group of twenty officers arrived in the east wing. They were suspected of being involved in the plot, and from what I could gather many of them belonged to General Fellgiebel's communications staff at the Wolf's Lair. They were the ones who should have isolated the Führer's headquarters. They were to pay dearly for their failure.

Working on the shower-room heating, I listened to their talk. It was quite incredible. They were relieved to be in Torgau, entirely reconciled to death, and were not perturbed at the prospect, as it would be an honourable end by shooting. Their philosophy baffled me, but I had not the heart to tell them that even these modest aspirations were unlikely to be realized, as the SS were now effectively in charge of Festung Zinna and were not concerned with honour or propriety.

Next morning my suspicions about what would happen to the twenty were confirmed by the arrival of three plain-clothed Gestapo interrogators. They set up their instruments of persuasion in a large communal cell situated on the second floor. The officers were interviewed one at a time, and the screams emerging from the cell were horrific. They did not bother the interrogators, who, in the mad world of Nazi Germany 1944, kept office hours: punctiliously arriving at nine and leaving at five. I assumed they lived in Torgau. Maybe they had their wives with them and were kind to children and animals.

Soon the condition of these twenty proud, valiant officers became pitiable. Some of them could no longer walk and had to be dragged from the interrogation room by the guards. Others pulled themselves along the corridor on their hands and knees, often leaving a trail of blood in their wake. Every so often one would be taken from the interrogation room to the death row and shot the next morning. Presumably he was reckoned to have told all he knew and was of no further use.

The prisoners' suffering was aggravated by the sadistic treatment they received from the Festung guards, eager to ingratiate themselves with the SS and in mortal fear — as were so many of the 'Home Front soldiers' — of being sent to the Eastern Front. The guards kicked these wretched prisoners just for fun. 'Give the bastard another one, Günther. That's right: put the boot in.' Cheers and hilarity all round.

Another favourite pastime was to bring a Ukrainian prisoner from the north wing to sweep up the blood from the Festung. These Ukrainians had volunteered to fight with the Germans, and were subject to German military discipline. But the discipline of the guards was far removed from Army Regulations. For the Ukrainians were ordered to remove the blood not with mop or cloth, but with their tongues.

'It tastes good, doesn't it, you bastard?' the guard would say. 'Lovely grub, eh?' When the victim remained silent he would be made to kneel with his face pressed to the floor. Then one of his tormentors would stamp his foot on the stubborn one's neck and smash his features to pulp.

The result was more blood.

'Now you can lick that up too.' Ultimately the wretched Ukrainian was forced to comply, whimpering, 'Yes, it's delicious. I like it. Give me some more.' The guards loved that. They referred to this performance as the 'tea party'.

Hauptmann Friedrich, hard man though he was, would never have countenanced such behaviour, but he was only in nominal command and did not even appear in the east wing while the Gestapo remained in residence.

Eventually one prisoner out of twenty remained. He took

everything the Gestapo could do to him and simply refused to talk. They could not break him, so in the end they decided to shoot him. He was only semi-conscious as they dragged him by the heels to the death row, deliberately letting his head thump cruelly on the concrete. All the while he kept repeating the same words: 'I tell you, I don't know, I don't know.' Maybe he was speaking the truth, but I hope and believe his courage gave the Gestapo their answer and that others lived because he died without talking.[1]

With the business of interrogation complete, the Gestapo agents left Festung Zinna. The east wing lapsed into sinister somnolence once more. In contrast, the north and west wings emptied — as their inmates went off to the heaven-bound battalions — only to be filled up straight away with fresh recruits. Many were now arriving from the Western Front, found guilty of desertion or of failing to hold ground. And this time not all were officers. A whole detachment of the Kriegsmarine — three hundred in all — were brought in because they refused to take their U-boats into the Atlantic where the British were sinking them with ease. Such deterioration in the morale of Germany's most formidable men betokened a more general collapse of the will. Whole battle units from the West, many of the soldiers still in battle gear, were sleeping out in the west rooms because the cells could not accommodate them. However, they were merely in transit. They stayed one night in Torgau and next morning moved out to the Special units and were promptly dispatched to suicide missions on the Russian front.

On a glorious September morning Festung Zinna came to attention for the arrival of a general. The guards lined up as though for inspection, eyes front, rigidly at attention. But this was no ceremonial visit. The general was a prisoner, accompanied by two officers of lower rank who shadowed him and were clearly his gaolers. The general was still imposing . The gilt on his epaulettes denoted a full Colonel-General — a rank commensurate with commanding an army — and at his neck glittered one of the Third Reich's highest awards for gallantry, the Ritterkreuz mit Eichenlaube, the Knight's Cross of the Iron Cross with golden oak leaves. The guards could not believe that such a godlike figure could be a prisoner. They positively goggled.

[1]Those conspirators who survived paid tribute to their comrades who endured extreme torture and gave nothing away.

So did I when I recognized him. As he approached me I was in no doubt that I had met him. He was one who had been present at the meeting between Die Wasserkante and the generals at Davoserstrasse, Berlin, the meeting which had failed to check the rift in the anti-Nazi movement. What's more the General recognized me; he gave me a flicker of acknowledgement as he passed.

That evening a business-like Hauptmann Friedrich called on me in my boiler-room haven. 'Kersten, do you play chess?'

'Yes, Herr Hauptmann, I'm an average player. Why do you ask?'

'Because,' he replied in a tone of proprietorial pride (and why not?), 'The General' — he appeared to put the two words in capitals — 'The General has informed me that you and he are acquainted.' Here his voice took on a note of sheer amazement. Then he shrugged. 'But I accept the General's word without question. He is a man of great integrity and highly respected throughout the Army. The General has expressed a wish to have a game of chess with you. Will you oblige, Kersten?'

Here was the German deference towards rank, particularly military rank, in its extreme form. The General was a prisoner. Strictly speaking, he was not entitled to rank or honour, and would assuredly lose both. Yet Hauptmann Friedrich was positively glowing at being on speaking terms with him. What a coup! What a privilege!

I was irresistibly reminded of the story of the Captain of Köpenick. Only the Germans could have been duped into handing over their town's treasure to a confidence trickster simply because he was dressed in a uniform of the Imperial German Army. Friedrich was as starry-eyed about entertaining a real *Generaloberst* as any young girl introduced to a famous film-star.

Hauptmann Friedrich was waiting expectantly for my answer. 'Why of course, Herr Hauptmann.' I replied 'It is true to say we are acquainted. I will be available — in about half an hour.'

'It is an honour to be asked, you know.' The Hauptmann smiled — even the acquaintance of a *Generaloberst* was worth a touch of obsequiousness.

At 19.00 hours I made my way to the top floor of the east wing. All the cell doors were closed except one — the last at the end of the corridor was open. The guards were on duty, but they respectfully kept away from the open door, presumably because their obvious presence might offend the General. The guards practically ushered me towards the Presence.

As I entered the cell the General rose and held out his hand. 'Erwin Jänecke. I recognized you all right.' We shook hands.

'My name is Jakob Kersten, Herr General,' I said. 'I've been in prison for a year — arrested September 1943 and I'm lucky to be alive.' I blurted out all at once.

'We must play chess, Kersten: to keep the guards happy. That is the reason you are here, understood?' And so began a relationship which gave me fresh insight into life at the military summit of the Third Reich.

We did play chess, night after night, but the games were nominal. Jänecke totally outclassed me. He was quite brilliant. After one or two visits he suggested to the guards we close the cell door 'to assist concentration'. They rushed to obey.

'So you wonder why I am here?' He raised his head from a study of the chess-board to give me his full attention. His mouth belied the rest of the face — frosty blue eyes over a prominent nose, and crowned by thick, greying brows — for it had a sardonic twist to it.

'You know, I was arrested on Hitler's personal orders. Quite an honour, really. You see, I directly violated a *Führerbefehl*, instructing me to hold on to the Crimea. The Führer had this idea that the Crimea should be a German Gibraltar, dominating the Black Sea, providing the Reich with an unsinkable aircraft-carrier from which to threaten the Soviet oil-wells in the Caucusus. He even sent me reinforcements when I hadn't asked for them — and this was when the Russians had already bypassed the Crimea. So I ignored the command to resist to the last man and conducted a strategic withdrawal.'

Jänecke had command of the Seventeenth Army in the Crimea. Despite heroic resistance — in which anti-Soviet Russians played a notable part — the peninsula became untenable. Jänecke and his forces were trapped in Sevastopol. The Nazi general Friedrich Schörner assured Hitler that the Crimea could be held. Jänecke told Hitler, by letter and in personal interviews, that it could not. Despite the Führer's unalterable resolve to hold on to the German foothold in the Crimea, Jänecke evacuated the troops from Sevastopol in May 1944, thereby saving 40,000 from his army's original strength of 134,000.

'But once you do that, you find out how "heroic" certain ambitious subordinates are.'

'Why, *they* would never think of withdrawing — for Führer and Fatherland to the end. I recall one of them — after being safely delivered behind German lines — quoting to me press descriptions of how German soldiers had risked all to get back into Stalingrad to join their comrades in a glorious death. Naturally, these reports found their way back to the Führer's headquarters. The honour of the Officer Corps stops short of promotion. Anyway, that has been my experience.'

He let his voice fall to a whisper. 'Hitler is quite insane, you know. His orders bear no relation to reality. He cannot conceive what it is like to fight without air cover, or with insufficient anti-tank guns or sure supply-lines. The troops in the East are ready to hold on beyond the normal bounds of human endurance, but they cannot perform miracles. So the commanders must pay the price, so that the reputation of the greatest military genius of all time may remain inviolate; so that the famous intuition is not tarnished.

'You'll be getting a lot more people in here soon,' he remarked chattily. 'Some like me who have defied a *Führerbefehl;* others who were too close to the recent *Attentat* for their own good.'

'Just what happened over the putsch, General?' I broke in.

'*Ach*, we Germans are poor revolutionaries, Kersten.'

But not, as the General was to discover, poor revenge-seekers. One night in October I arrived for our regular chess match to find him stripped of his decorations and insignia. He gently reminded me that while I continued to address him as 'General' he would be shot as a private. The German Army did not shoot generals.

That evening Jänecke dropped his guard and openly abused many of his fellow-officers.

'They only wanted to know about the conspiracy, Kersten,' he muttered savagely, 'after the conspirators had won. I thought we would have Guderian on our side. He ended up as Hitler's man. You know all about that in Torgau.'

'So you think he betrayed us?'

'Don't you?'

'Well, why didn't he give away the whole plot — Stauffenberg, the bomb, everything?'

'Because he didn't have all the information,' explained Jänecke. 'The inner circle — maybe twenty officers at the most — decided to execute Hitler; the time, the place, the method was a closely guarded secret. The rest of us thought Hitler would be held prisoner: we never imagined he would be assassinated. Never. We'd taken our oath of loyalty to him.'

This confirmed the impression I'd got from Hofacker's bold oration. There had been no mention then of killing Hitler.

'You must understand, Kersten,' he went on, 'that commanders such as Rommel would not have countenanced murder. If Hitler died accidentally, so to speak, well then a different situation would have existed and Rommel would have gone along with the conspiracy. He was already committed to seeking peace in the West when he was wounded. The failure after that lay with his fellow-officers.'

'Kluge?' I asked.

'Him, yes. But Clever Hans was always a fence-sitter. He had an arse of iron. He was one of the soldiers your man — another Hans, wasn't it? — warned me of at the meeting you attended.' He grinned. 'You were quite overawed then, weren't you?' I nodded. 'And now you calmly play chess with a *Generaloberst.*' He paused. 'Well, with a former *Generaloberst;* such is progress.'

'But if it wasn't Kluge who failed in the West, who was it?'

The General smiled gently and played out fool's mate on the board. As he transported the black queen to the mating square he looked up: 'In my opinion it was his Chief of Staff.'

'Speidel?'

'Yes. He could have imposed his will on Rommel's staff and brought Kluge round — or arrested him. Speidel was at the centre of the web. He should have used his knowledge and his power to greater effect. Now?' he shrugged. 'God alone is aware of what will happen to Rommel. It was Speidel who used Rommel's HQ quite shamelessly to advance the plot. Rommel cannot escape the consequences.

'Remember, Kersten, everything, in the end, hinged on the West. If our commander had offered to surrender, and had publicly acknowledged this readiness, the Anglo- American democracies — whatever their arrangements with Stalin — could not have turned it down. The pressure from public opinion would have been too great. But once our people in the West wavered . . .' He lifted his hands, palms upturned, and sighed.

Next evening the General casually told me, 'Tomorrow I go to Berlin. So this is goodbye.'

'Will they execute you?'

'That I do not know. I will stand trial, but where they intend to hold the wake is their concern.' I never saw Generaloberst Jänecke again.[1]

As high-ranking German officers flooded in to the east wing of Festung Zinna, Hauptmann Friedrich became almost blasé. He quite lost his veneration at seeing at close quarters the glittering epaulettes and the claret stripe on the trouser-leg that denoted the staff officer. Too often this claret was accompanied by a red line under the officer's name on the ticket outside his cell. That red line denoted the death sentence. Why get blood pressure over what would soon be cold meat?

Yet occasionally Friedrich would revert to his old-fashioned Prussian reverence to someone of rank; as in the visit of the Baroness.

One day I heard a woman's voice. I couldn't believe my ears; more than a year had elapsed since I'd encountered a woman.

'Is my husband in this part?' The voice was cultured, authoritative — and deeply sad.

'Certainly, madame.' Hauptmann Friedrich sounded like a maître d'hotel. 'On the third floor. . . this way . . .'

I glanced over the railings to the ground floor. There was the Hauptmann and a finely dressed woman coming up the central staircase. I watched them slowly move past me. I heard the Hauptmann say, 'We are almost there.' He didn't glance in my direction, but the woman, middle-aged, carrying herself straight-backed, smiled. They stopped outside the seventh cell, and Friedrich ordered the guard to unlock it. The Hauptmann ushered the woman in. 'Thirty minutes is all the time allowed, I'm afraid, Baroness.' There were three prisoners in that cell. All 'vons'. All titled. And all under sentence of death.

Twenty minutes passed and the rest of the prisoners on that floor returned from exercises. They hung around chatting — as most of them were to be shot, discipline swiftly relaxed — and a few moments later the guard returned to tell the Baroness she must leave. A number of prisoners recognized her as she moved towards the central staircase. One after another called out, 'Tell my mother [or my wife] I am in Torgau.'

She broke. Tears streamed down her face and she covered it in her hands. She sobbed bitterly, and swaying, gasping and crying, she rushed towards the main exit. The voices of the con-

---

[1]Jänecke was imprisoned in Eastern Germany and captured by the Russians. He was repatriated in 1958.

demned followed her. 'Tell my mother . . . tell my wife . . .'

Years later I recalled that scene as one of the most vivid in my life. It reminded me of films I'd seen about the French Revolution.

I never discovered who she was. Hauptmann Friedrich said she was 'a friend of a friend'. He would divulge no more.

Seventeen

Preparing for Defeat

Across Europe the search for traitors and defeatists continued remorselessly. Some of those on the outskirts of the plot had remarkable escapes. Hans von Herwarth should have reported to resistance elements in Salzburg. But the message to do so never reached him. He had returned, exhausted, from a trip to General von Niedermayer's old division in Italy. To allow him a complete rest his wife told the conspirators (she did not, of course, know they were conspirators) that he had not yet come back. So Herwarth escaped involvement in the 20 July coup: as did his chief General Köstring. To keep out of the limelight Köstring and Herwarth quit the centre of affairs in Berlin for the relative calm of Belgrade. Had the worst come to the worst they could have slipped off to surrender to one or other of the factions fighting the Germans. What held them back from any such venture was the near certainty that their families would suffer in retaliation for their desertion.

This nightmare anxiety kept many German officers in line, doing their duty, obeying the craziest orders right to the finish. A few, however, disregarded personal considerations in order to save their men. On occasions even SS commanders were prepared to risk everything that fate and a demented Führer could throw at them, in order to spare their soldiers. General Bocham led his troops from doomed Oberglagau — and was cashiered. Colonel Gonmell let young officer cadets escape from beleaguered Poznan — and committed suicide rather than face the disgrace awaiting him.

While SS officers of a humanitarian turn of mind dared not let themselves fall into Russian hands — immediate execution or worse would have been their lot — no such inhibitions affected the pro-Russian generals of the Wehrmacht.

General Dewitz-Krebs resolved to bring closer the war's end by surrendering himself and his soldiers to Tito's partisans at Banja-Laka in Yugoslavia. Josip Broz — who had adopted the pseudonym Tito to deceive the pre-war Yugoslavian authorities — was a communist. But like all the other factions in his country — Serbian nationalists, Croatian nationalists and royalists — he was not above doing deals to help him preserve his position. So poor General Dewitz-Krebs found himself exchanged for high-ranking partisans and back in Germany, where he was promptly tried before the Reichskriegsgericht and sent to Torgau to await the verdict. Thus began the last chapter of Torgau's bloody role as the graveyard of the German officer class.

Ernst, our friendly guard, who kept the news network fully supplied, was the one who brought us news of Dewitz-Krebs's presence.

'Hey, Dutchman, there are two more generals,' Ernst announced in the manner of a man building up a high-class clientele. 'Their names are von Dewitz-Krebs and von Niedermayer,' he added, stressing the 'vons'.

'Repeat the names, Ernst,' I gulped, aware that my voice shook, while I could feel the blood draining from my face.

'Von Dewitz-Krebs and von Niedermayer. Is anything wrong?'

'No, no,' I answered, striving to calm the rising terror. 'It's simply that the last name rings a bell. I'm sure I've read some books by him.[1] That's how I remember his name. Interesting.' I hoped that would be enough to satisfy him, for he was looking at me strangely. Finally he nodded and went off, and I could release the emotions boiling up inside me.

'My God,' I said aloud. Niedermayer was Die Wasserkante's man at the top of the Wehrmacht, and Dewitz-Krebs had been at the Berlin meeting with Niedermayer, Hans and myself! I rubbed my wet palms on my trousers. Was this the beginning of a round-up of Die Wasserkante and its associates? Would they be coming for me?

It was ridiculous, of course. Why should the leaders betray me, even under torture? But I had been through so much, and had then relaxed, so now that dangers crowded in again I panicked. I

[1]Niedermayer did indeed write books — about his First World War exploits and his travels in the Near East.

had to know how things stood. I rushed off to the top floor of the east wing where high-ranking officers were always held. I looked at the names at each cell and deliberately slowed my walk to a casual pace.

I arrived at the cell marked 'von Dewitz-Krebs' and tried the door. Not surprisingly, it was locked. The guard looked hard at me. 'Yes?'

'Could you open the door? I have a repair job to do on the central heating.' My heart was beating so loudly I was sure he could hear it. Why was he staring at me? Had Krebs talked already?

Wordlessly the guard bent over the lock and opened the door. I nearly fell into the cell. And there was von Dewitz-Krebs. Smiling. He was untouched. Fair, slightly greying hair in place, blue eyes unclouded, no shadows of suffering. Thank God. Thank God. He came towards me, arms outstretched.

'I'm pleased to see you. A friendly face is unusual these days. Sit down.' He motioned me to a seat on the other side of the table from which he'd risen. He could see from my obvious distress that I wasn't visiting him to inquire about his health.

'Calm yourself, my dear fellow. My arrest has nothing to do with your activities. Tell me, what's your name?'

I told him. 'Well, Kersten, my present confinement is due to a routine omission today in the Wehrmacht — failure to obey a *Führerbefehl*. I am awaiting the sentence now, and have no doubt I will be executed.'

I tried to reassure him that others who had retreated, such as General Graf von Sponeck, who had withdrawn from Kertch, had been spared.[1]

He refused to be comforted. 'You must remember, Kersten, I *surrendered* — and to communist bandits at that, for such is how Germany officially regards Tito's partisans. How can I possibly be permitted to survive?'

He lowered his voice still further. 'You and your kind are right. Russia is going to win the war, and if we have any future it must be in partnership with them. After that meeting — the one in Berlin — I cut my links with the conspirators. They were far too pro-West. I even' — he grinned weakly — 'made contact with Wehrmacht officers sympathetic to negotiations with the Soviet

[1]Sponeck was, however, executed before the war's end.

Union. I heard rumours that there had actually been talks between the Russians and the Germans. But nothing came of it. No officers were prepared to risk their lives to let in Ivan.

'The curse of this war, Kersten, is that there is so much bitterness. Such terrible hatreds. A general can surrender in Yugoslavia with his division. But if a sergeant puts up his hands he will be shot — after he has been forced to tell all he knows. Then come the reprisals. Ah,' he shuddered, 'guerrilla war, the worst kind there is. And mark me, Kersten, Germany will have to pay for this devil's brew. If these fools had tried to buy off Moscow instead of making up to London and Washington we could have spared the Fatherland much suffering. Now the Russians will come, and they will not be forgiving. Still, you will be on the winning side. For me, I think it will be too late.'

Sc' of the officers who had attended the Davoserstrasse conference, Schwanenfeld, Hofacker, von Hase, von Tresckow — the active plotters — were dead. Jänecke, Niedermayer and Dewitz-Krebs were in prison. So was I. That left Hans and one or two others whose names and fates were unknown to me. On that record my chances of enduring seemed pretty small.

For the moment, however, I was reassured. I took leave of Krebs to search out the man whom I hero-worshipped: the boss, General Oskar Ritter von Niedermayer.

He was easy to find, next cell but one to Krebs, and his door was half open. I raised my tool bag, nodded towards the cell and the guard nodded his assent. Yet I was too much in awe of the great man to just walk in. I knocked.

'Come,' said the familiar voice.

He stood by the table, as commanding as ever but much thinner than I remembered. His uniform was bereft of decorations.

'So,' he cried with genuine pleasure, 'it is Karl.' (He recalled my code name!)

'Good afternoon, General. Or may I call you Professor?'

'You may indeed.' He gestured to his tunic, where patches of lighter shade denoted the removal of medal ribbons. 'It would perhaps be more accurate. As far as I know they have not taken my academic title from me.'

'You have not been tried? Like . . . ?' I gestured in the direction of Dewitz-Krebs's cell.

'Not by the Kriegesgericht, but I have been dismissed the Army by the Honour Court, and am due to appear before the

Volksgericht, the People's Court, in Berlin.' It was because he had not yet been found guilty that he was allowed the luxury of an open door.

He motioned me to close it to, though not shut it completely. We sat opposite one another. He looked steadily at me. 'You look well, Karl.'

'And you too, Professor. How does it come that you are here?'

He lent back and brushed his hand through his hair. 'Folly, sheer damned folly. After all these years of leading a double life, up to my eyes in a Marxist underground, I fall victim to a momentary loss of self-control. I talked out of turn.'

My questioning gaze prompted him to explain. 'Earlier this year I was put in command of Russian volunteers on the Western Front. The Wehrmacht ranks had filled with ex-Soviet prisoners. I tried to improve their lot, although I bitterly resented their attitude. Never mind. It is not my job to sentimentalize. When the Soviets come they will doubtless have their own methods of dealing with defectors.

'As I was saying, from July onward, my command was extremely mobile as we tried to keep one step ahead of the advancing Americans. What a contrast to the Eastern Front! I remember when the Ivans would come at us with hardly any artillery preparation across open country and through minefields. With the Allies there is a terrifying aerial bombardment, followed by artillery, followed by tanks. They certainly let you know they are coming. My men had little stomach for the fight.'

'So you are here because you refused to stand your ground . . .'

'Don't interrupt, Karl.' The tone, cool, authoritative, caused me to blush in shame. 'Our Führer doesn't expect his sub-human Russian levies to fight, so there is no *Führerbefehl* requiring us to "yield not one inch". In fact Adolf Hitler still believes that Russians cannot fight, despite all the evidence to the contrary.

'No, I fell from grace because I spoke my mind. In the Caucusus and later when I trained troops near Liegnitz I knew which officers I could speak to frankly. I was careful, naturally, never to utter a word about our association. On the progress of the war, however, I talked with those whom I reckoned were not mere Goebbels gramophones. With my command in France I made a mistake. We were at Metz when, tired and hot and sick to death of constant Allied bombing — you cannot move by day — I ventured to suggest to some of my staff officers that we would shortly be going east again, and soon we would bump into the Russians. I discovered I had not picked my company when the military police arrived. Two of my staff had denounced me for defeatism.

'I was much too afraid for Die Wasserkante to make a great noise in my own defence. Better by far to be accused of something that matters little than to betray a great cause. I am the only one who will be in the dock. If I ever reach there. For the war's end surely cannot long be delayed.'

'How,' . . . I paused. I wanted to ask about Inge and Hans and Oma Jansen and the Bremen ring and what the movement would do when victory was ours, but Niedermayer had read what was in my mind, and his eyes vetoed such questions.

'How . . . is your family?'

'Well. They seem to be reasonably safe from the bombing in Bavaria.'

'And your own family?' he asked.

'I never really had one,' I answered, and again there rose the overwhelming desire to ask about Inge. Suppressing it, I gently enquired about the Putsch.

'My dear Karl, you should know more about that than I do. It was here in Torgau that the plotters lost out. I only have information on the matter because we have a local civilian worker in the Festung: Otto.'

'Of course.' Otto had made himself known to me, but I had avoided him as much as possible. He was pretty low-grade and I didn't want to involve myself with someone I didn't wholly trust, and also I wasn't keen to work for Die Wasserkante inside the Festung. Otto clearly carried news and gossip to the outside — he went home every evening at 18.00 hours.

'We were betrayed,' I murmured.

'Not we, Karl,' Niedermayer interjected, 'the generals. And they were betrayed by their own kind. Like everyone, I received Guderian's general order[1] telling us all to be good little National Socialists. And the common talk — from Model,[2] for instance — was that Guderian had shopped the Torgau conspiracy. The

[1] Of 25 July 1944.

[2] Field Marshal Walter Model replaced Kluge as Commander-in-Chief West in 1944. He committed suicide in the following April when he was encircled by the Allies in the Ruhr.

generals are unanimous now in pledging their loyalty to the Führer.'

'So we were right . . .'

He held up a warning hand. I fell silent, and we turned to inconsequential talk. Shortly afterwards I left. But I was able to visit him frequently in the following weeks because Hauptmann Friedrich was most impressed that I was well acquainted with so distinguished a man — and one, moreover, under whom Friedrich had briefly studied when Niedermayer was professor of geopolitics in Berlin.

Festung Zinna had at this period in the winter of 1944-45 returned to normal: that is, regular executions and swift transportation of the less serious prisoners to penal battalions on the Eastern Front. Torgau was a transit camp to eternity. But as the SS were not present Hauptmann Friedrich was able to run the prison on routine lines.

So I was left free to wander in my capacity as heating engineer. One cell I visited held a British captain who had escaped from Colditz — some twenty kilometres away — and was presumably about to be returned there. His own unforgettable service was to give me an English cigarette. After our usual ersatz German ones it nearly blew my lungs out.

British tobacco marked my first adjustment to a post-war situation. Festung Zinna was adjusting too. The guards started to behave most reasonably. Oh, they still shot whomsoever they were ordered to, but the zest had gone out of their work. They no longer dealt with prisoners as bits of rubbish to be shovelled into the earth. They treated even the condemned with some dignity.

Fear of defeat prompted this new humanity — but fear of the Russians was the palpable, overwhelming, factor. Torgau lies in the eastern part of Germany, and though we had no knowledge at that time of how the Allies proposed to partition the Reich we were pretty sure the Russians would get here first — they were already on the Vistula, less than four hundred kilometres away.

Ernst was the first guard to ask me, 'What do you think will happen if the Russians come, Dutchman?' He was careful to say 'if' and to whisper his question. Had he been overheard muttering defeatist talk it would have been a *Himmelfahrt,* a heaven-bound commando for him, regardless of his crippled leg. I would have enjoyed his reaction had I drawn my finger across my throat but I didn't want to provoke him. If he, or any of the others, imagined I posed a threat to them because of what I could tell the Russians I would not see another dawn. I simply shrugged and replied that I had no idea.

Triumphant radio broadcasts at Christmas announcing German victories in the West during Rundstedt's Ardennes offensive brought no joy to the guards of Torgau.

'What the hell are they doing attacking in the West when all the troops are needed in the East?' was the prevailing grumble in the canteen when I went to repair a radiator. They ignored my presence, and I was able to gauge the despair in their voices. These men had wives and families, probably in Torgau itself or near by. German propaganda was working overtime to convince the people that victory was the only alternative to a holocaust in which German women would be turned over to ravenous Mongols; men would be castrated, and the youth indoctrinated to Bolshevism. The propaganda found a real response when the Soviets, following the launch of their January 1945 offensive, broke into East Prussia.

Now at last the war was on German soil, and reports began to filter back of horrifying atrocities. When villages were recaptured Goebbels's press photographers would picture ravaged farmsteads and ravished women and the bodies of hanged Nazis. These pictures and the harrowing stories of those who had endured 'Bolshevik barbarity' had a profound impact on the guards at Torgau, as, no doubt, on the rest of the population. The fact that the Germans had perpetrated ghastlier crimes, and on a far vaster scale, on Russia in no manner lessened this sense of outrage and a growing resolve that it must not happen here.

One freezing late January day Ernst came into the boiler-house (strangely, we still had ample supplies of solid fuel at Torgau) and remarked in a tone of utter despair, 'Do you know, Dutchman, these bloody Ivans are raping women of eighty?' I was sure this was a typical Goebbels frightener, and a whopping lie, but caution made me answer, 'My God, are they?'

'I'm shit scared,' continued Ernst. 'If I get a chance it's me for the West.'

'But you won't get a chance.' I blurted out.

'What do you mean?'

'Well, you'll have to do your duty as a soldier of the Reich right to the bitter end.'

He said nothing, then his face reddened. 'If they come — the

Russians, like — will you say a good word for me? I always treated you decent.'

The end must be near, I thought. I assured Ernst that he could count on me.

Shortly afterwards Hauptmann Friedrich came to see me. While the rest of us got thinner and thinner — not surprisingly, on a diet of acorn coffee, black bread, bean soup and cabbage — the Hauptmann got fatter and fatter. He had an odd request to make.

'You get round the Festung more than most, Kersten.'

'Correct, Herr Hauptmann.'

'Sometimes you know more than is good for you and see more than you should.'

I remained silent.

He came to the point. 'This has nothing to do with you directly, but I want you to tell me the names of the guards who co-operated with the three Gestapo men, the torturers.'

Again caution counselled me. 'But I'm no informer, Herr Hauptmann, just a heating engineer.'

'Come now, Kersten,' Friedrich grunted. 'You will not place yourself in any jeopardy. You know the position. We must get rid of unsavoury elements.'

'What will you do with them if I tell you?'

'I cannot charge them, but I intend to transfer them to Transport Command, which will require them to take supplies right up to the front line — the Eastern Front. It is not a pleasant posting by any means.'

Memories of the sadists kicking the prisoners, forcing the Ukrainians to lick the blood off the concrete, stirred me. With a real satisfaction I spat out the names: Hauptfeldwebel-major Günther and Feldwebel Sisco.

'Good. That will be all Kersten.'

So Hauptmann Friedrich was clearing the decks, polishing up his image preparatory to handing over to the victorious allies. But which Allies? The Red Army or the Anglo-Americans? Would Hauptmann Friedrich and his kind survive if the Red Flag unfurled above Torgau? What future would Germany have under a Soviet administration? With the Russians advancing at the pace they had set, and the Western powers still sitting on their arses on the wrong side of the Rhine, I was convinced the Russians would win the race. I had to see Niedermayer.

I was on my way there when I met an excited Ernst. 'We have another general.' He was positively gloating. 'Hans Speidel,'[1] and he stood back proudly. So what? I thought. I was becoming blasé about generals, especially defeated ones. Ernst was quite dejected by my reaction. 'And,' he added, eager to recover his reputation as news gatherer for the grapevine, 'he has been interviewed by Kaltenbrunner[2] and Gehlen[3]' This did draw me up abruptly. Kaltenbrunner, the black uniformed giant with the duelling scar was a figure to inspire terror. Gehlen I had never heard of, but presumed both were at Torgau to investigate Speidel. I had a whole agenda for talks with Niedermayer who spoke of his hopes of the coming rapprochment with Russia.

'Good evening, Herr General.'

It was uncanny. Here we were sitting in one of the tightest security prisons in Germany: a senior officer of the Wehrmacht facing execution for criticizing Hitler and a glorified janitor, both members of a Red resistance group and happily discussing post-war reconstruction. The door was closed, and by habit we still kept our voices low. But in February 1945 almost everyone in Germany was adjusting: guards, prisoners, Hauptmann Friedrich.

Niedermayer was today a non-person; degraded by the Army's Court of Honour. Tomorrow he would — despite his modest disclaimers — be a major power in the land. A glow of confidence, mixed with pride at being close to the great, suffused me — and after all, I would surely share in the power and the glory too.

'Tell me . . . (I almost said 'Oskar', taking him at his word that we were equals, but checked myself in time), Herr General, how did you get away with it for so long? I mean . . . the organization, the movement . . . and your position in the Army?'

Had I overstepped my privileges? No one who had not spent years close to the German military establishment can envisage the awe which uniformed authority engendered. Even now with

---

[1]Chief of Staff to Army Group B in the West. Removed from command in September 1944 for suspicion of complicity in plot against Hitler. After the war became Commander of the West German Army.

[2]Ernst Kaltenbrunner, Chief of Reich Security Services, was executed as a war criminal.

[3]Reinhard Gehlen, head of Fremde Heere Ost, intelligence on foreign armies of the east, principally the Soviet Army. Helped to rebuild the West German army after the war.

Niedermayer seated at a bare deal table in a bleak prison cell, I was metaphorically at attention. Moreover, he had made a point of never mentioning Die Wasserkante's affairs.

The General looked coldly at me. The blue eyes held more than a touch of frost. Then he relented and for the first time since we had met in the Festung he used that ever so German gesture, the pointing index finger, vigorously waved.

'A year ago, Kersten, I might have had you shot for asking such a damned question. Today things are different.

'Nothing is easier in Germany than doing something illegal under cover of a uniform. You are acquainted with the Captain of Köpenick?' I nodded. 'Very well, I applied that camouflage on a grander scale for a nobler cause. So did others of similar rank. Officers of comparatively humble rank were also able to influence events because they were men of aristocratic birth who were, shall we say, born to rule. It is no secret — they have all been executed or are about to be anyway — that German Military Intelligence was honeycombed with anti-Nazis, thanks to the head of the Abwehr.[1] But these were pro-Western officers. They did nothing to hinder the Nazi efforts in the East. They were as opposed to Communist Russia as they were to Hitler. But the fact is they operated a kind of subterranean service parallel with their official duties. And because they wore uniforms and commanded rank and breeding, they remained immune. The Nazis are terrible snobs — or at least they were until the *Attentat*. Today it is safer to pretend National Socialist zeal and sound proletarian principles: that is, if you still believe Hitler has a chance of winning the war.

'For myself and my comrades,[2] we adopted the same cover as the Westerners. We never contemplated betraying them, but if they had found out what *we* were up to I do not think they would have been so understanding.'

'But how,' I interposed, 'could you' — I searched for words — 'turn the course of events?'

'In a hundred ways. At staff conferences, informal meetings, in private conversations you suggest plans, policies, courses of action that will have the opposite effect to promoting Nazi

[1] Admiral Wilhelm Canaris, executed on Hitler's orders, April 1945.

[2] An account of the Soviet spy ring in Switzerland, *La guerre a été gagnée en Suisse*, says ten Bavarian officers rose to high position and betrayed military secrets to the Soviets. Niedermayer and Müller were Bavarians.

interests. We were able to operate quite effectively in that fashion in the Caucusus.'

He was no longer really talking to me (the references to the Caucusus were away above my head), he was reminiscing, rehearsing his memoirs or maybe simply getting it out of his system lest he be eliminated before the war's end.

'The strength of Die —' he paused — 'our organisation has been that we operated indirectly instead of those others,[1] which made direct contact.' He gestured vaguely towards the East.

'We were always small compared with the Western Group, but we could count on a few of the old Bismarckians.' He shifted his gaze from the table to my blank, uncomprehending face and laughed.

'By old Bismarckians I refer to German officers who held to Prince Bismarck's nineteenth-century policy of keeping on good terms with the Russians. There are still quite a few of them. Which, my dear Kersten, is further confirmation that the German officer class will not be liquidated when Ivan arrives. We Easterners are far too important, truly necessary to Moscow.' The last phrase was whispered as though he was trying to reassure himself.

'It might have gone differently.' — He had resumed his confident tone — 'if Stauffenberg had brought it off. He was consumed with ambition, that one — but he would have been a formidable figure to stand up for Germany, even defeated Germany, against the Allies and the Russians. Who is left today? Speidel? There's an odd one. He went before the Honours Court before me and was acquitted. Yet Keitel passed on the Führer's view that Speidel should be found guilty. Now you tell me he is here. He remains in custody and remains safe. Out of sight, out of mind.

'And what has he handed over to Kaltenbrunner? Maybe nothing. But then why are they leaving him alone, when everyone knows he was implicated in the plot?

'Lucky Speidel. If I go before Butcher Freisler[2] I will cease to have any interest in politics. Now let us play chess.'

---

[1]The Schulze-Boysen group and the Red Orchestra underground.

[2]Roland Freisler presided over the People's Court and invariably sentenced the accused to death. He was killed in a British air raid on 3 February, 1945 — and his death had an important bearing on those awaiting trial. (Von Schlabrendorff, for instance, was enabled to survive, and write his memoirs.)

Eighteen

The End of Torgau

The net was tightening. On 8 March the Western Allies crossed the Rhine and the drive into the heart of Germany from east and west reached towards its climax. We joked that the Allies and the Russians would meet in Torgau[1], but before then what would happen? Would Festung Zinna simply be forgotten, its prisoners left to their own fate?

A sinister answer arrived in the form of cartloads of convicts from civilian gaols who were packed into the west wing, under an SS Sturmführer. The SS man was a big, bronzed, well-filled fellow, a credit to his smart uniform. The prisoners, clad in blue and white striped garb, were so emaciated that their ears seemed their most notable features. They stuck out from their skeleton faces like bats' wings. And they were laughing!

Hard labour for these creatures must have been a living death, so when they were 'freed' for front-line service they had grabbed the opportunity. Now, true to Prussian form, the convicts were to declare themselves 'volunteers.'

'Heil Hitler' bellowed the SS man, not forgetting to click his heels in perfect synchrony with the raised arm. His dark eyes gazed expressionlessly on his two hundred volunteers. 'Germany needs you,' he cried in a penetrating and authoritative and rather cultured voice. 'We need soldiers. The Führer is willing to give you a chance to prove yourselves. You will fight together with the SS for the future of Germay.' Naturally, there was not a single refusal.

Lost, bewildered, shorn of personality as well as hair (they

[1]They did. Torgau marked the first junction between Soviet and American troops.

were almost bald, so closely had they been cropped), it is doubtful if they even understood the message. These criminals — thieves, rapists, murderers whose execution had somehow been overlooked — were to fight for Germany alongside the SS, Nazi Germany's élite, the aristocracy of merit, the best blood of the *Herrenvolk* — there could be no sharper irony and no stronger proof of how near was Germany's defeat.

The comb-out expanded at an alarming rate. Once more the black shadow of the SS darkened Torgau. Every cell door was flung open and the inmates asked, 'How long is your sentence?' If it was less than ten years the SS man would ask, 'Are you willing to volunteer for front-line service, to fight for Führer and Fatherland?' No one refused. By next morning Festung Zinna was emptied of another huge batch. Sooner or later, and sooner rather than later, they would be coming for me.

Russian auxiliaries, who were in Torgau for mutiny, were not exempt from the offer no one refused. Known as Vlassovites from their commander General Vlassov (who had defected to Germany), they were tough and truculent. General Köstring, who was in complete control of the Soviet dissidents, had won Himmler's permission to recruit as many as would serve. He arrived at Festung Zinna to win back as many of these lost sheep as he could. Köstring really cared about his Ivans, but in this instance he was unsuccessful. They rejected his appeals, preferring to take their chance in Torgau to certain death on the battlefield. They were to find they had chosen the worst of all possible worlds.

Stay or go? My mind was made up by our fuel situation. At long last Festung Zinna was running out of coal. Within a week our reserves would be exhausted, and since milder weather was on the way — it was late March — I would lose my precious function, my reason for existence. Not even a sympathetic Hauptmann Friedrich would be able to save me then — I would probably be casually shot by one of the SS men clearing out the cells. I had the eerie and certain conviction that no one was going to survive Torgau.

My opportunity came when a regular Army lieutenant arrived to organize FGAs — *Feldgefangenerabteilungen*, field penal units — for southern Hungary.

At this stage of the war, with the Russians shelling the outskirts of Berlin and the Western Allies mopping up the Ruhr, Adolf Hitler from his bunker was still concerned about holding on to distant territory and arranging for a counter-offensive. So penal battalions had to be sent to prepare fortifications or clear minefields, or whatever fatal tasks were allotted them. It was a front-line version of the bomb-clearing of Naumburg. Well, I had emerged from that, so why not Hungary? And I had an evil precognition about Torgau's fate.

The lieutenant was quite definite: 'You should leave; this will not be a pleasant place to be in.'

'But how do I leave?' I protested.

'There is a transport leaving for Hungary in two days. If you wish I will simply include your name on the list of those who will travel.'

A few months before he would never have dared deviate from strict military regulations — unless he had been a very out-of-the-ordinary officer. But now, with Germany disintegrating, all kinds of crazy things were happening: deserters were being hanged from lamp-posts to drive home the message 'total war requires total obedience', and at the same time junior officers were forging generals' signatures on movement orders. Fanaticism to the point of madness, coupled with the most blatant cynicism: that was Germany in the spring of 1945.

I decided to go. I went to see Hauptmann Friedrich to get his permission. I had the distinct impression that he was about to leave too — unofficially. He knew all about the fuel position, and as he said to me, he had no intention of waiting in a freezing Festung for the Russians or the SS to polish him off. He gave his permission, waved us away and actually expressed the hope that we would see one another after the war. For a man who had tried to have me killed he showed a touching faith in the healing power of forgiveness.

Ernst, next on my list of leave-taking, tried to argue me round. 'We'll be safe in Torgau. The journey to Hungary will be hell. You'll never make it.' I patted him on the shoulder and assured him that I would. 'I hope you make it too,' I added.

My final call was to von Niedermayer. He was alone, playing chess. He agreed I should get out. He was waiting himself to be posted to Berlin, or held just outside the capital for his long-delayed trial before the People's Court. The German mills of justice ground on as *Götterdämmerung* approached.

'Good luck, Kersten,' he said in cheerful military style. 'I hope you meet up with Inge again. You deserve some happiness. Give her and Hans my thanks and best wishes for the future. I am going to miss you, but we shall meet up when this is over.' We shook hands. I never saw him again.

At 04.00 hours the following morning I boarded the train for Hungary. Nearly four hundred men were herded into nine closed goods wagons. The last wagon was reserved for the guards. I was in the centre of the train, and in the centre of the prisoners. We stood upright, arms pressed to our sides with two tiny ventilation shafts and a journey of five hundred miles before us.

Men opened their bowels where they stood: they vomited and fainted — and stood because they had nowhere to fall. The stench was unbearable. The drumming throb of the train hammered into the brain, and some fellows called to God, to Christ, to Mother. Or simply cursed. Time ceased to have any meaning. The train rolled on and on until one lived the rhythm of the wheels and had no other existence.

The doors could not be opened from within, but were bolted on the outside.

My mind wanted in some ways to be mesmerized by the rhythmic beat of the wheels, but nevertheless it refused to submit. Instead it travelled over the past, and I became angrier and angrier at the prospect of ending my life in stinking suffocation. Nobody now was speaking a word — not because they had lapsed into mute acceptance, but because the only way to breathe was through your mouth: if you breathed through your nose you would throw up.

Collective madness would, I'm sure, have been our fate, and mutual strangulation our remedy, had Russian planes not appeared on the scene, and their cannon shells sliced the wooden planks of the wagons. I reckoned they were Russian because we were so close to the Eastern Front.

My luck held. I was in the middle of the wagon, and so my companions absorbed the sharpened slivers of wood and the bullets that ripped through us as the Russians began strafing us. Bodies pressed in on me as prisoner after prisoner sagged at the knees. Corpses are difficult things to deal with at the best of times — I'd handled quite a few — but when you are powerless to hold them off they are the very devil.

God in heaven, I thought, I'm going to drown in flesh and blood.

The train had stopped, yet still the Russians continued to send their bullets and shells into the carriages although no one was returning their fire. Kill! Kill! Kill! was how it was in these last weeks of the war. Years of death and destruction had anaesthetized humanity. A twitch of life invited a bullet.

At last — presumably they had run out of ammunition or fuel — the planes pulled back. The screams of engines and exploding ammunition were replaced by the anguished cries of the dying — no longer worried about breathing through their noses.

Many minutes passed. I tried to count the seconds, but I gave up in despair. I thought we were going to be left to die. Then I heard the outside bolts being drawn. The doors were flung open and a rasping voice yelled, *'Raus! Raus! Alles raus!'*

Only a German soldier of the old school could order the dead to dismount. The blast of fresh air revived me as I pushed bodies aside, clambered over the dying and fell out of the wagon. The stench of putrefaction was appalling. I hadn't realized how swiftly human flesh could decompose in severe humidity and when crushed by other corpses.

Four of us emerged from my wagon. It transpired that only thirty from the entire train-load of four hundred had survived the attack, and some of them were appallingly injured.

'Get in line, get in line.' We unhappy few shuffled into a semblance of order, and I saw to my dismay that two of the guards were Günther and Sisco, the ones I had reported to Hauptmann Friedrich. So this had been their transport duty!

Presently an SS Sturmbannführer drove up in a staff car. He took one look at our ragged band and decided he wanted none of us in his district of Oberpullendorf. Sharply he ordered Sisco and Günther, the senior surviving NCOs, to 'march these prisoners out of my territory at once'. His driver slammed the car into gear and drove off. We marched away. The wounded and dying were left to fend for themselves.

We marched westward. At this point in the war every German soldier or civilian with any freedom of movement marched towards the advancing British and Americans.

On and on we marched, painfully dragging one leg after the other. We were hungry and weak and thankful for the soft rain which wetted our parched lips. Hour after hour we tramped Hauptfeldwebel Günther informed us that a dysentery sufferer had a simple process to follow. He could run to the head of the column, drop his trousers, empty his bowels and catch up with the rear of the column. If he wasn't ready to fall into line as the column passed he would be shot. 'We will wait for no man,' bellowed Günther.

To give the Germans their due, they still managed to pull out efficient service in the midst of total collapse. We were creatures with a function to perform, therefore we had to be fed — just. So horse-drawn Army kitchens duly pulled up and each of us received a bowl of hot soup and a single piece of brown bread. This happened once each day.

On the fourth day we seven survivors — the others having died or been shot — met up with another group of prisoners who had halted beside a mobile kitchen. Günther and Sisco seemed almost sad at giving up command to the Hauptmann in charge of the bigger group, which numbered seventy or eighty men. Günther and Sisco enjoyed seeing how many of their charges could last out. 'We only want *men* to march with us,' they had jeered. Now they too would have to take orders.

On we went, led by the Hauptmann astride a skinny skewbald. We passed a signpost. We were heading towards Purgstall. That night, for the first time since the train strafing, we slept under cover in a farm shed. Early next morning an SS officer arrived and commandeered forty of our members for some undisclosed front-line duty.

We were getting extremely close to the front now; the rumble of guns becoming louder and louder.

Our Hauptmann and his ten guards were not at all anxious to reach the fighting, so we wandered in circles. One of the prisoners cried out that this was his home countryside. He broke ranks and shuffled off towards a farm. Günther let him get thirty metres and then drilled him neatly in the back. 'Right on target,' he remarked.

We buried him eighteen inches deep. We were too tired to dig further.

On the fifth day the Hauptmann took half the prisoners and half the guards and left the remainder — myself included — under the care of Günther and Sisco. We were ordered to move ourselves towards St Pölten in Austria and place ourselves at the disposal of the first Wehrmacht officer we came across. The Hauptmann and his charges then vanished. So, next day, did two of our guards. By voluntarily absenting themselves from the war they risked summary court martial and execution within thirty minutes of being captured. On the other hand, they obviously reckoned the odds favoured being captured by the Allies.

Sisco called us together and said, 'It's all over. Decide for yourselves where you want to go.' We stood about, wholly lost. Sisco, Günther and the other guard were just as bewildered. Captors and captured alike had no idea what to do next, so we did nothing. We hadn't the sense to sit down, just stood shuffling our feet and looking down at what remained of our boots.

Then it happened. Round a bend in the road hurtled a car with a big white star on the bonnet and an American Negro soldier at the wheel. The car screeched to a halt, and while a turret-mounted machine-gun covered us, two of the jeep's three-man crew leaped out. They surveyed us with a mixture of surprise and amusement. I was fascinated by their flashing white teeth.

'Say, man, what goes on?' I could understand English, but was hopeless at speaking it. One of the other prisoners explained in halting fashion. The two Negroes smiled hugely.

Günther turned his head. 'I am in charge here,' pointing a finger at himself.

'You *were* in charge,' countered the American. 'You had your day, boss.' The other Negro turned to us prisoners. 'You take their guns now.' We stood stock-still, unable to grasp the change in our situation. 'Take their guns, man' shouted the Negro, pushing one of the prisoners on the shoulder. 'Go on, it's your ball game.' That phrase meant nothing (though it stuck in my mind as none other had ever done), but we got the meaning all the same. In seconds we had seized the guards' arms.

'Well done, men. You have things to do, so we'll just go back up the road for a while. Be back in maybe twenty minutes.' And pointing a finger at Günther, he said 'For sure man, the war is really over for you.'

At this something cracked inside Günther. To be captured by white Anglo-Saxons was one thing; to be taken by Black men quite another.

It was too much for this man, sergeant-major of the Master Race. He spat. The Negro stepped forward and grabbed Günther by the collar. The Negro's teeth gleamed now in rage. Then he flung his prisoner from him and nodded to us.

A moment later, to a screech of tyres and grinding gears, the jeep disappeared round the corner from where it had arrived.

Günther raised himself to his knees and looked piteously at the avenging ring. Sisco stood silent, at attention. I held one of the rifles. I wanted to prolong Günther's agony — I looked closely at him. He had closed his eyes, screwed up his face and, oddly, was holding his hands over his ears as though he could not bear to hear the sound of his own death.

Our turn now. A volley of shots rang out, bullet after bullet went into the writhing bodies. We pumped them in long after they were dead, and then we tossed the corpses into a little stream near by. They floated away, and my first thought was 'I'm glad I didn't stay at Torgau.'

Ten years passed before I heard a first-hand account of what happened at Festung Zinna a few days before the Russian and American armies met there. The bloody finale sealed the compact made between Martin Bormann and Heinz Guderian to limit damage to the reputation of the Wehrmacht as the price of its complete integration into the National Socialist state.

It was pure chance, and a cold easterly wind, which forced me to seek shelter and warmth in one of the small bars in Cuxhaven on the North Sea in November 1955. I had settled myself in one of the deep-seated cubicles when I noticed, or rather heard, something which I could never forget — an uneven scraping. I looked up and there was Ernst, my guard and confidant of Torgau. He was a shrivelled figure, a gaunt shadow of the man I'd known at Festung Zinna, but undoubtedly Ernst. I called his name.

He stopped immediately, slowly turning round and looking at me in astonishment, his watery eyes staring without recognition. He took a few steps towards me, dragging his leg and stooping lower than I had remembered. He peered at me.

'Who are you? Nobody in these parts has called my name for years.'

'Ernst, remember Torgau, the prison Festung Zinna? Remember the Dutchman in charge of the central heating?'

His face lit up. 'My God, you are the Dutchman. You made it! You survived! We were told at Torgau that all the prisoners on that transport had been killed.'

He sat down on the other side of the table, a shabby worn-out man, old beyond his years, and told me what had happened.

'You had been gone about a fortnight, maybe more, when the

end came to Torgau. My God, Dutchman, you were bloody lucky you took that train to Hungary.' (I allowed myself a faint grin.) 'It was 20 April, Hitler's birthday: I remember that because we'd been listening to Goebbels babbling about true victory belonging to those who followed their leader with blind devotion — and this, mind you, when we could hear Ivan's guns and the Allies were racing to get as far east as they could, against no opposition.'

A trace of impatience on my face brought him back to the point of his narrative.

'Yes, well, the SS Sturmbannführer turned up again, this time commanding a dozen or so SS troops and about fifty Hitler Jugend. Boys, mostly — sixteen or seventeen — but each of them had seen front-line service, and eight or more were wearing the EK2.[1]

His eyes had a faraway look; he was reliving every minute now. 'They looked angelic: blond hair occasionally flopping over one eye; blue eyes, naturally; firm jaw-line — real little Aryan heroes. But, by God, we soon found out that each of these little bastards carried more authority than any of the Army officers including Hauptmann Friedrich.'

'I thought he would have been out of Zinna by then,' I interposed.

'He couldn't make up his mind,' replied Ernst. 'He was so used to taking orders, he couldn't give one to himself.'

'Anyway,' he went on, 'we heard the SS toughs had come from the concentration camp at Oranienburg and had been specially selected for the assignment.'

'They made no secret of the fact that they were to bring about the final solution of the Torgau problem. At that time we thought you had all perished on the train journey to Hungary.'

'Nearly right, Ernst. Only five of us survived out of four hundred.'

'So . . . you can thank your lucky stars the SS didn't know of that. They'd have followed you right into the Allies' prison camps to get you.'

I smiled disbelievingly.

'Yes, they would,' he insisted.

'All right, all right,' I soothed him. 'Get back to Torgau.'

[1] Iron Cross, second class.

'When the guards were ordered to assemble in the Festung Yard, in full battle-order and all, we assumed the SS were doing their *Himmelfahrt* act. We need volunteers — you, you and you. The only ones to be exempted were people like myself who had been badly disabled. We were told to carry on with our normal duties.

'Sure enough, we watched the usual pantomime. The SS officer making the usual "for Führer and Fatherland" speech, then the guards were ordered to come to attention and marched out under the command of an Oberscharführer. From what followed, I'm not sure if they even reached the front to die as heroes. I think they were probably shot. Can't say for certain, of course, but I never heard of them again.'

'So why are you here?' I asked.

'Same as you. Pure bloody chance.' He undid the buttons of his grubby shirt, displaying an ugly red scar on his chest. 'I was twice wounded: once in France and once in Russia. But this, Dutchman,' he pointed to the scar, 'was done by my own countrymen, kids young enough to be my sons.

'The Hitler Youth shot every one of us guards who remained at Zinna. They left me for dead — dumped in the river Elbe, so I was told later. I knew damn all about it; when I came to in a temporary hospital under control of the American Forces I was told a woman had rescued me, taken me to her home and nursed me. Saved my life; but to this day I don't know her name or where she came from.'

'And Hauptmann Friedrich?'

'Last I saw of him he had been locked away in death row.'

'Friedrich!'

'Yes. The SS checked the files and I heard the SS commander — you couldn't help hearing him, he was screaming at the top of his voice — shout "We are here to eliminate the lot, you fat swine, not to safeguard you for your friends, the Americans." Then he ordered his SS men, "Take away this garbage before I vomit." And off went Friedrich under escort to the ground floor of the east wing.'

'The death cells?'

'Exactly.'

'And the prisoners, what happened to them?' Ernst looked down at the table and clasped his hands as though in prayer. I was sure it was to stop them shaking. He appeared to be about to burst into tears.

Afraid of doing anything emotional that would precipitate a breakdown, I pushed my own glass of brandy to him and commanded 'Drink'. He swallowed it in one. I ordered another two and waited. He downed both of them. I thought he might find it difficult to articulate, but, strangely, the drink seemed to have sobered him.

'I'll never forget. It is like a nightmare, coming back to me night after night, reminding me of my own execution.' He made an obvious effort to get a grip on himself.

'You thought the Army guards of Torgau were vicious murderers and sadistic bastards, Dutchman. So they were. Most of them. And whether they died under Russian guns or were killed by the SS machine pistols I'd weep no tears for them. But you should have seen those little lads of the Hitler Jugend — they made the old guard look like plaster saints.

'I don't know how to describe them. They were . . . it was as though they were filled with religious fervour, or drugged out of their minds. They just went crazy.

'They'd clearly been told the prisoners were the scum of the earth, the dregs who were pulling down the great Third Reich. The guards, like me, and administrators, like Friedrich, were the property of the SS who were clearly working to a prescribed plan; no evidence, no pack drill. But the Hitler Jugend boys were on the rampage. Their hatred for those poor bastards in the cells was something else again.

'You'd have thought the prisoners had raped their mothers, so personal . . . so individual was their rage. It boiled. The SS concentration camp men gave them expert advice on the process of liquidation, but the boys added their very own brand of passion. If Hitler had had another couple of million like them, the Nazis would never have lost the war.

'Anyway, they dragged the prisoners from their cells on the ground floor and shot them. But on the upper floor they gave themselves a special thrill. They fastened the end of a rope to the railings, and the other end was slipped round the neck of the victim. Then one, two, three and over he went. The jerk when the rope became taut removed the head from the body. Blood spurted everywhere as though there was a pump working.'

'You witnessed all this?' I interposed.

'Of course. We were called to witness it. Part of our education.

As we were going to be killed anyway, it didn't make much difference. The SS kept their machine pistols pointed in our general direction, though they were so fascinated by the executions that they didn't watch us closely.

'As I was saying, every time a head bounced on the lower landing, the cry would go up: "Another traitor gone!" It was an orgy. I saw it all through a haze of sickness and fear, so I couldn't identify the prisoners, but I remember as they dragged another forward to fix the rope the Hitler Jugend screamed — or chanted, rather — "All of you have to go. No enemy of the Führer and the Reich will survive. We'll see to that."

'Headless corpses, bullet-ridden corpses: Zinna was like a slaughterhouse. When the berserk murder was at its height Friedrich's deputy, an Oberleutnant, tried to intervene. He appeared from somewhere — an office, I suppose — shouting to stop it, stop it! The SS commander drew out his revolver and shot the Oberleutnant at point-blank range, shouting *"Für Wehrkraftzersetzung"*[1] as he did so.'

Ernst's voice faded to a whisper. 'I fought on two fronts. I never saw sights like I saw in Zinna, and to see your own countrymen slaughtered as animals — by your own countrymen! Oh, God! Pray that never happens to you, Dutchman.'

His voice picked up once more. 'When they had disposed of all the ordinary prisoners they proceeded to turn their attention to our remaining general (was there just a hint of the old proprietorial pride?) — Generalmajor Karl von Dewitz-Krebs.

'The Hitler Jugend leader, a boy of sixteen, I guess, seemed to be well-informed about the General's trial in Berlin. He told his platoon, "This man is a principal traitor to Germany and an enemy of our Führer. It is his kind who have betrayed our great ideals. The orders are that he shall not fall into enemy hands alive."

'Six of us were detailed to step forward and officially "witness" the execution. Maybe generals expect that kind of formality. But, Dutchman, it wasn't a proper execution. Whether deliberately or through inexperience or over-excitement, the firing squad sprayed the poor bastard with bullets that maimed but didn't kill. He twitched and jerked even after he was on the ground. Then, when he lay still, they clicked their heels, gave the Nazi salute

[1]For undermining defence strength.

in lovely calm, clear voices pronounced "*Heil Hitler. Es lebe Deutschland.*"

'Afterwards the Vlassov fellows were told to clear up the mess.'

'What happened to them?' I asked.

'To the Vlassovites? No idea. Reckon they were eliminated too, but whether by the Russians who would shoot them as traitors or by the SS or HJ, I just don't know.

'They were still around when the SS polished us off. And that, Dutchman, is how the end came to Torgau — and bloody nearly to me too.'

The sardonic last remark seemed to restore his equilibrium. He rose, pressing me back in my seat when I suggested he might like another drink.

'No, Dutchman. Maybe it did me good to get all this out of me when it's been bottled up for ten years, but I don't want to go on. I hope we don't meet again. I don't want any reminders.'

We shook hands. He left without saying goodbye.

Nineteen

'The Price was too High'

For me the war was over. Guarded by our friendly Negro soldiers and a white American, we few survivors were transported to a camp in a small, beautiful valley two kilometres south of Kematen.

The Americans had achieved a miracle of organization and improvization. Not only did they accommodate their own men — for them too the war was over, as they had reached the limit of their eastward advance, in conformity with the secret Allied-Soviet agreement — but they swiftly adapted to cater for thousands of prisoners too.

It was marvellous, unbelievable, to be back in civilization, to be treated like a human being, given a name, and addressed in good-humoured fashion. There was plenty of excellent food, washrooms, clean blankets. We were provided with a change of clothing and first-class medical attention. It was a wonderland. The Americans seemed to have everything. They could have drowned the Germans in ice-cream.

After two or three days I felt a new man. Then I noticed a strange and disturbing sight. Armed German soldiers were being drilled by their own officers, and this was clearly approved by their American captors. German civilians in the camp were exuberantly certain about what prompted these manoeuvres. 'The Americans will not stop at Berlin,' they exulted. 'They are going to drive the Ivans all the way back to Stalingrad, and to do that, of course, they need us Germans to help them.'

This was the old Goebbels talk: that the alliance between the capitalist Western Allies and the communist East was bound to break down, and that as soon as their armies met they would start fighting one another. I recalled how Hans and Inge had forecast that the end of the war would see a vast ideological chasm open which would ultimately lead to a new war. Were the Americans starting it before the old one ended?

Then a couple of days later the Americans and Russians did meet. At Torgau! And instead of fighting we were shown newspaper pictures of happy GIs dancing with robust Red Army women. Joy and camaraderie were unconfined. Clearly the Americans had simply been keeping their captives busy.

The news came that Hitler was dead. For us who had been prisoners of the Nazis that truly marked the end of the war, even though a skeleton government carried on the struggle for another week or so.

Adolf Hitler was National Socialism. The Government projected his prejudices, ideas and instincts. For twelve years he had been the embodiment of Germany, the absolute leader. 'Adolf Hitler Is Victory' proclaimed the posters showing a steely-eyed Führer gazing into a visionary future.

'Ein Reich, Ein Volk, Ein Führer' was for millions of Germans a wholly acceptable substitute for The Way, The Truth and The Light. They had put their fate in the hands of a man who in seven short years had raised Germany from the depths of despair to the mastery of Europe. All that had gone wrong was due to the perfidy of England, the wiliness of the Jew and the sheer mass brutality of Bolshevik Russia. No blame was attached to the beloved Führer who, according to the official broadcast, had 'fallen at the head of the troops'. (No mention then of Eva Braun and the suicide pact.)

The ordinary German prisoners were thunderstruck. The SS men — and we had the best part of a Waffen SS division in camp — simply couldn't believe it. 'The Führer dead? Nonsense!'

But with the Wehrmacht's unconditional surrender, the most fanatical and bigoted had to accept reality. The fight went out of every German serviceman. They just wanted to go home.

Taking advantage of this deflated mood, the Americans opened the gates and told all the prisoners — officers as well as men, SS as well as Wehrmacht — to 'Git'. The result was a mass exodus with men going off in all directions. I was both relieved and outraged; relieved at being free for the first time for five years; outraged that the SS were getting away scot-free.

I was preparing to quit when I was told to report to the

Administrative Office. I had expected some such call, because the Americans were naturally interested in me, and a bit suspicious of a Dutchman imprisoned in one of Germany's top-security military prisons. They suspected, rightly, that I was a political and they wanted to know more.

So I duly reported to an office sparsely furnished but decorated — yet again! — with a flag; the Stars and Stripes. A lieutenant — I never did get his name, though I believe I heard him referred to as Grumbach — was seated behind the inevitable plain deal desk holding an inevitable manila-covered file. He was an easy-going type: one leg up on the table, tie loosened, shrewd yet humorous eyes, a mouth always ready to split into an Eisenhower-size grin. He spoke perfect German (his parents had emigrated to the USA from the Fatherland), but no one could have offered a greater contrast to the conventional German military figure than this relaxed Yank.

He began by asking me questions about my politics. After some skirmishing, I admitted outright that I was committed to the Left. 'And what do you intend to do about that?' I demanded.

At this period, having been long withdrawn from the world, I had no idea how the Americans would react. I knew nothing of the West's love affair with Joseph Stalin, 'Uncle Joe' as he was depicted in the newspapers and the cinema screens of Britain and America. From what little I had seen, and from what Inge, Oma Jansen, Hans and Niedermayer had told me, America was Russia's natural foe. So I was wary and resentful.

'I don't give a damn about your political alignment,' replied the lieutenant. 'I am attached to the OSS.' He recognized my blank stare and explained, 'The Office of Strategic Services, intelligence work. It's my job to track down Nazi war criminals. I suspect some of them will try to make their way through to Italy, and I have reason to believe they may travel by way of Lambach, here in Austria. I need men to watch for these people; men who will fit in unobtrusively with the local scene and who are' — he paused — 'unequivocally anti-Nazi. You meet the bill. Are you willing to help?'

'Look here, Lieutenant,' I said, 'if you are so eager to track down Nazis as you say you are, why have you set free half a division of the SS?'

'I am not interested in small fry. I am only after the men at the top. So will you help?'

Now if I could persuade the Lieutenant of the OSS to find Inge for me . . .

'Is something wrong?' he inquired.

'I wish to track someone down for myself.'

'Who is he?'

'It's not a he. It's a she.'

'Is she so important?'

'Very important to me, yes,' I resumed, 'I have already told you I was attached to a left-wing organization. Well, she was my senior partner. She was principal secretary in the Gestapo HQ in Bremen.'

'Really, how interesting! What was her name?'

'Inge Werner.'

'I'll tell you what' . . . But before he could tell me anything I told him what to expect.

'If you will use the resources within your organization to find Inge Werner, I will gladly assist you to track down the Nazis.'

He stretched out both hands to shake on the deal. 'Well done, Kersten, we'll get started straight away.'

Shortly afterwards I found myself on the lower slopes of the Alps in the Lambach district. I was dressed in Austrian national costume to espy Nazi fugitives. Frankly I could not have cared less who was escaping. I found no evidence of a planned route, and quickly forgot all about any so-called duties.

The weather was good — late May — the scenery was magnificent and I was intent on enjoying myself and my freedom. It had been arranged that I would work on a farm where help of any kind was welcomed. So I got myself established on a fair-sized farm where the owner was a former Nazi burgomeister, a certain Herr Emathinger.

He was a decent fellow who made me very much at home. Married, he had a son who had not yet returned from the war and two daughters. His wife was . . . well, not a shrew, but a highly hysterical woman who had not come to grips with defeat.

I worked in the fields, from dawn to dusk, and enjoyed every minute of it. Until, or unless, you have been in prison you cannot imagine the joy of the open air; the breeze in your face, the sun on your back and the smell of the earth. It was intoxicating.

My prison pallor changed to a ruddy glow. I worked in the fields digging, draining, feeding the cows and eating fit to burst. As was the case in most of wartime Europe, folk in the countryside filled their bellies while townspeople near starved. The war gave a tremendous boost to depressed European agriculture, and with transport disrupted, much of the food stayed on the farm. Anyway, you made far more money on the black market (how ironic to find Negroes and Jews saving the Aryan *Herrenvolk!*), so while the townies begged or sold their bodies for cigarettes — the only currency of value — we country bumpkins lived on the fat of the land.

Of course, I never caught any escaping Nazis. I never bothered to look for them. The most unpleasant people that I met, in fact, were professional Nazi-hunters.

One day a jeep drew up in the yard and two strapping young fellows stepped out. The heftiest of the two called for Burgomeister Emathinger. 'We're Austrian Freedom Fighters, members of the local resistance' (it was news to me that Austria *had* any freedom fighters).

'What does that mean?' said the Burgomeister, by now looking thoroughly anxious.

'We have come to take you and your wife to internment. You will be sent to a camp.'

Dear God, I thought, it is starting again, only this time the swaggering young men are wearing the arm-bands of the anti-Nazi movement.

'What crime have we committed?' asked the Burgomeister nervously.

'Two,' came the reply. 'You, Burgomeister, were a member of the Nazi Party and your wife spat in the face of an American pilot.'

At this point the Burgomeister's wife, an aggressive woman at the best of times, joined in before her husband could stop her.

'Yes, I did,' she declared in a shrill voice. 'He was a bomber pilot who had dropped all his bombs on Vienna. His plane caught fire. I watched it . . . He bailed out over our land. He was lucky I only spat at him. He was a terror airman, a killer of women and children . . .' She rattled on while the bombastic 'freedom fighters' struck attitudes and finally stopped the wife's gushings with a blunt 'Shut your mouth, woman. You are coming with us. We are the liberators.'

Europe was liberation mad, and some of the liberators were worse than the men from whom they were liberating us. The two grabbed the Burgomeister and wife and hustled them into the jeep. 'Please stay with my daughters,' cried Emathinger as the jeep drove off. 'I'll help all I can,' I shouted above the roar of the engine.

It was as well I stayed to work on the farm and look after the two girls, for no sooner had one branch of the newly-founded Freedom Front left than another arrived. These two were armed, or at least one was, and they said they were Czechs seeking Nazi criminals and any food and valuables they could pick up by way of confiscation, or 'liberation'.

'These are daughters of Nazis,' said the pistol-carrier. 'We can take from them whatever we want.'

I noticed that he was holding the gun sloppily, and that the safety catch was on. I advanced on them, glowering and confident.

'Keep your distance!' squealed the gunman. I struck with my right foot, and the pistol soared over his head. Then I grabbed his right arm, swung it round and dislocated it from the socket. His partner dived at me, and I had the pleasure of kicking him in the face. I picked up the gun and, muttering about shooting them like dogs, watched as they raced from the house, bolting like frightened rabbits.

Nonchalantly I assured the girls there had been no danger, as I received their breathless praise with assured modesty. 'Come, I will demonstrate to you that the weapon is harmless.' I aimed the pistol at the door, pulled the trigger — and the gun went off! It was I who nearly fainted! Obviously the safety catch was faulty. No wonder the 'freedom fighters' had run! I emptied the magazine and buried the cartridges.

In accordance with previously made arrangements I met the American lieutenant every Monday in the market-place at Lambach.

At last he had news for me. 'We've found Inge Werner.'

My heart almost stopped beating. 'Where?' I gasped.

'In Bremen. In a nursing-home. She is gravely ill. It appears from information from our OSS detachment there — Bremen, remember, is in the British zone — that the Gestapo discovered her involvement in the Resistance. That was only two days before the city fell, but it was enough. She's been viciously tortured. I don't know the full details, but that is the gist of the message we received this morning.'

Stunned, I remained silent.

'We don't want you to leave Lambach yet,' the lieutenant broke in. 'When the time is ripe we'll lay on transport; probably when the captain is going up to liaise with the British and visit OSS detachments. Meanwhile stay at the farm.'

The OSS I knew, could get me to Bremen, which I would never reach under my own steam, so I agreed to remain at the farm and leave unobtrusively when I received a message to do so.

It was not long in coming. I slipped away from the farm and the lieutenant picked me up at the crossroads. We drove to an airfield on the outskirts of Linz where the captain was waiting for his aircraft to take him north.

No sooner were we airborne than the captain told me how Inge had been found.

'She was discovered in a routine check by British troops, lying in a cellar in a house in the centre of the city. Presumably she had been left for dead, or to extend her dying as long as possible. A British staff sergeant had her moved to a military hospital, and, because of our . . . mmm . . . interest in you and your politics we had her transferred to our own small nursing-home. I think it is only fair to tell you how extensive her injuries are. You agree? You want to hear everything?'

'Go ahead,' I replied.

The captain breathed deeply, then launched into a litany of cruelty, delivered in a monotone as though he was making a situation report.

'Well, every major bone in her body is broken. Some in more than one place. There are extensive bruises to the face and injuries to the skull. Her arms, hands and legs have been twisted out of shape and bear signs of being badly burned. She has internal abdominal injuries which were not diagnosed until later and which are likely to prove the most serious of all.'

I could not recognize my own voice. It was metallic, as though I were an automaton.

'You're absolutely sure you've got Inge?'

'Absolutely. We made our own inquiries, and checked with captured Gestapo officials — small fry — who have identified her as their former chief secretary. There is no doubt whatsoever that the patient we have is Inge Werner. She's in a small private ward, by the way. The least we could do for one of the very few heroines of the German resistance.'

The last phrase sounded as though he'd rehearsed it.

'Anything more?' I asked dully.

'Well, when she was found she was in a coma. She is now fully conscious, and, with excellent care, the broken bones and bruises are yielding to treatment. However, the internal injuries are of a different order, and I think it would be best to let the doctors explain them to you. Apparently they consider it was a miracle she was still alive when the British patrol came across her.' He paused. 'I think you should brace yourself for a pretty terrible shock. The end, Kersten, may not be far off.'

I couldn't and I wouldn't believe the captain. 'She'll recover.'

He chose to ignore that. 'When she was delirious she kept repeating a phrase. I have it here.' He pulled out a wallet and removed a scrap of paper. *'Hans lass dich grüssen.'* She repeated it over and over again. I assume it is some sort of code.'

'It is.'

'By the way, Kersten, the doctors report that she seems to be waiting for someone; almost certainly you. They reckon this anticipation is keeping her going. She's said nothing up till — since she became fully conscious, I mean. Your appearance could prove the catalyst.'

I judged that the captain's principal purpose in reuniting me with Inge was to acquire as much information as he could about the Left-wing movement in West Germany. The OSS was already planning for the future. The Gestapo belonged to the past.

Once in Bremen the captain and I were driven directly to the military nursing-home. I was shattered at what I saw. The whole place was bombed flat. Here and there a family shuffled along pushing a pram or small wooden cart carrying their entire belongings. Whether they were going anywhere — possibly to a relative with comparatively undamaged property — or whether they were simply moving for the sake of doing something was impossible to tell. The only motor traffic on the road belonged to the British military. Their soldiers didn't look at all exultant, as you might have expected them to do. They appeared upset at the devastation and misery caused by their fellow-countrymen of the RAF.

What Germans I saw were pathetic, broken and anxious to please. One or two saluted our jeep as it raced along. To think the Allies had given themselves nightmares at the prospect of guerrilla warfare against Goebbels's phantom 'Werewolves'. The

Germans I saw wouldn't have resisted a budgerigar.

'God knows how long it will take to rebuild this,' I remarked, gazing round.

'It's a lesson the Germans will never forget, that's for sure,' said the captain, sounding a lot less concerned about the Germans and a good deal more satisfied with the extent of destruction than seemed the case with the British. Maybe the English for all their 'we are an island' talk felt more the dreadful wounds of Europe than did the Americans from three thousand miles away. Any philosophical speculation on my part ceased as we drew up in front of what appeared to be the only undamaged building in Bremen — the nursing-home.

The Sister in charge told me that Inge spent most of her days sitting in a wheel chair by the window looking out over what remained of the city.

'She is awake now,' said the Sister, 'if you will come this way I will take you to see her.'

'No, please,' I answered. 'I would rather go alone.'

I climbed the stairs to the first floor, slowly and reliving our lives, hoping for the best, fearing — and believing — the worst. I began to regret that Inge had ever been found. A happy memory is preferable to hideous reality, and, judging from what I had been told, that was what I was going to find. At that point I nearly turned round to run out of the hospital. Instinct told me I would never forgive myself. So, bracing myself, I marched to the door and, without knocking, entered.

She sat in a wheelchair facing, not the window but the door: as though she had a premonition of a visitor. I would never have recognized her. Indeed, I had to stop myself recoiling in horror.

The doctors had shaved her head in order to treat the injuries to her skull. Her face was a mass of yellow bruises. Her body was twisted, her limbs unnatural. She was an old woman.

Inge recognized me instantly. She tried to rise, and fell back with a groan of pain. She tried to smile, but the ruined muscles of her mouth turned the smile into a grotesque grimace. The only part of her I could recognize was her eyes. They still lit up, full of love and understanding.

Standing above her, I bent down and she raised her left hand shakily for me to kiss. Tears trickled down her cheeks; in a husky, barely audible voice she murmured, 'Speak to me.'

I took both her hands in mine and felt sick at heart. Every one of her finger-nails had been ripped out. She saw my expression and nodded towards her feet, which were heavily bandaged. 'The toes are the same,' she whispered.

'Inge, my love, who did this to you?' I had one aim: revenge.

She gave me a long hard stare, exploring every line in my face. Slowly, painfully, she spoke: 'It is too late to seek revenge. Try to forget what has happened. I am not in great pain and I don't think I will have to suffer much longer. Please go away from Germany and find yourself a new life.'

'Get some rest, Inge,' I replied. 'I will be back tomorrow.'

I did return, and she talked for hours and hours.

'Did you know Oma Jansen and Hans are both dead?' She said this quite conversationally as if she were talking about the weather. She was standing back, looking at her own life in retrospect — and she wasn't yet thirty.

Hans had been killed in an air raid early in 1944; Oma Jansen had died of natural causes some time later. I had suspected she hadn't had long to live. But Hans and Oma didn't interest me at the moment. I looked into Inge's ravaged face.

'Tell me who tortured you. Describe him.' She looked away, her expression — in so far as she was able to express anything — reproachful. 'Please wheel me over to the window.' I did so. She feebly raised her left arm a little and pointed to the ruins of Bremen.

'Look at that.' I stared out at the frightening desolation. It was as though God had taken a hammer and smashed everything to bits. 'You know what they call this year of 1945 in Germany? The Year Zero. Nothing is left. We could never have built our freedom, our future, our happiness on that.' Her fingers fluttered towards the vista of rubble. 'The price is too high. Too high for us.'

I noticed a tape recorder at her side. 'What's that for?' I asked.

'Oh, the Americans brought it in. They were very anxious to establish my identity; who I worked for in the Resistance; how I managed to fool the Gestapo for so long. They were very kind.'

'I bet they were,' I thought, recalling the humorous eyes and shrewd questioning of my OSS lieutenant. The American approach reminded me of the Aesop fable of the man with the overcoat. When the wind tried to tear it off him he wrapped it round himself all the tighter, but when the sun shone benignly he gladly took it off. The triumph of persuasion over force.

'Did you tell them anything?' I remarked casually.

She gave a grimace, her nearest thing to a smile. 'I couldn't speak.' She sighed, and her shoulders slumped. Inge Werner, my vibrant, fighting, wonderful Inge, was swiftly giving up.

I leaned over her. 'See you tomorrow, my darling,' and slipped out the door.

As I approached the hospital exit the Sister in charge of Inge's room intercepted me. 'The doctor would like a word with you, Herr Kersten. Please come this way.'

She showed me into a small room crammed with filing cabinets between which a tiny desk cowered. The doctor, young and exhausted, was seated on the desk top.

'Herr Kersten? I believe you are a very' — he paused — 'long-standing friend of Fräulein Inge Werner?' I nodded 'Very well, I will whitewash nothing and hold nothing back. You are aware that she has internal abdominal injuries. We have been unable to stop the internal haemorrhaging, and, to complicate matters still further, septicaemia has set in. We can do no more for her. I am sorry.' He stood up. 'The brutal fact is that, in medical terms, it is a miracle that Inge is still alive. The end is only a matter of time, and not much of that.'

I was stunned. I could not accept that Inge's implacable will would be broken.

'But how . . . how?'

'There is no doubt at all how the injuries were inflicted,' replied the doctor briskly. 'Everyone who has examined her is of the same opinion. The internal injuries were inflicted by means of a broken bottle. This instrument was thrust deep into the vagina. It ripped open the neck of the womb. So there you have it.'

His brusqueness was part of the man-to-man approach. He had imbibed, very early on, the mental dismissal of torture, degradation and death so typical of Germany in Year Zero. He was clearly anxious to be off on other business. I thanked him briefly for his diagnosis.

Day by day Inge grew progressively weaker. I kept on pressing her to tell me who had done it and how she had been discovered. In the end I had my way.

The Gestapo agents who tortured her were just professionals; not known to her. One had spoken with a strong Austrian accent, a nondescript man of about forty. The other had been younger, in his late twenties, speaking with a cultured voice with a slight

Bavarian accent. He had gone for her private parts; the other for more conventional battery.

She told it all in halting, increasingly faint yet matter-of-fact fashion. After all, she'd lived with the Gestapo for years. Its horrors had become routine. In the collapsing Reich, pain was normal. She thought she'd probably told them everything, but, of course, it availed them nothing. The British were practically in the outskirts of the city.

'But how did they break your cover?' I asked.

'I never wanted to tell you this, darling,' she whispered, and those marvellous eyes misted over. 'I only made one mistake and that was the letter I wrote to the prison authorities in Torgau, attached to the file of Jakob Kersten. It was on Gestapo notepaper headed "Secret". It said he was to be treated as a civilian and was not to be permitted to go outside the walls of Festung Zinna. This was to prevent you being dispatched to a field punishment unit or death battalion. I signed the letter on behalf of Gruppenführer Müller.'

'And then?' I pressed.

'Then', she sighed, 'I suppose it was discovered by the last assault of the SS on the Festung — after you had left for Hungary — when they went through all your files. They came across the letter protecting Jakob Kersten. Kersten was an enemy of the Reich — otherwise he could not be in Torgau — and anyone who protected him, especially a secretary signing such a document on behalf of Gestapo Müller, must be doubly suspect.

'Everyone was suspect in those last days, my dear. It was as though a final madness of destruction encompassed those in authority. I was questioned formally, then subjected to interrogation: no sleep, or rather just the beginning of sleep, before being wakened again. Then stripped and beaten and then,' — she sobbed and turned her head — 'the ultimate refinements.'

Gradually Inge lapsed into delirium. Time and again she repeated Die Wasserkante's code phrase *'Hans lass dich grüssen'*. On my ninth day in Bremen she slipped away, leaving me with one last message 'The price was too high'. I folded her arms across her chest and murmured, *'Hans lass dich grüssen'*. Relief mingled with grief. Inge Werner, twenty-nine years of age, would not suffer any more.

Twenty

Death at Vladimir

Inge's death signified for me the end of my active service with Die Wasserkante. I did not hear through my 'godparents', those who had introduced me to the movement, that most had survived. But with Inge, Niedermayer, Hans, Oma Jansen and Hartoch gone I had no stomach for further espionage or courier work.

Moreover, against whom was it supposed to be directed? The great enemy, Nazism, lay dead at our feet. I ignored suggestions that the capitalist West was now the foe. If they were, as the movement's politicos declared, the successors to fascism in their opposition to the Soviet Union, why had they not driven ahead, driven eastward when they had the chance? Why had America not threatened the Soviet Union with atomic oblivion when Washington had the monopoly of the atomic bomb?

I could not see the tired, worried British, yearning to leave Bremen for Blighty, or the loose-limbed, slouching, anything-but-military Yanks, as the successors to Hitler's legions. Even if their rulers had wanted them to take on Russia I do not believe the Allied soldiers I met and saw would have done so. They were, for the most part, very pro-Soviet, having been taught for four years that Uncle Joe Stalin was the saviour of civilization. They just wanted to go home. So why should we of Die Wasserkante, who owed our liberation to the Western powers, work against them? I do not know how many of my comrades came to the same decision as I did, for under the closed-cell system I knew very few anyway, but it would have surprised me if many followed the promptings of the politicos. Though there were some exceptions . . . such as one Klaus Fuchs. The son of a Protestant but communist pastor, Fuchs was an active Die Wasserkante recruit long before the war, and fled to England at the age of twenty-one. There he began his work of research into the atomic bomb, and became part of the British contingent joining the Manhattan Project in the USA, a project which yielded the nuclear weapons that smashed Japan into surrender.

For six years, between 1940 and 1946, Fuchs passed on secrets to Moscow, and when the British finally unmasked him he was sentenced to fourteen years in prison. He was freed after serving only part of his sentence, and went to live in East Germany.

Klaus Fuchs represented the kind of dedicated, brilliant, intellectually convinced communist that I never was. He paid, in his own way, for his fate. But at least he was spared the ghastliness of life under the Swastika. Maybe if he had experienced it he would not have been so fanatical in service to another land of totalitarianism.

That is speculation. I never met Fuchs, but he sprang from the same political loins as those who founded Die Wasserkante as a protest against Kaiser militarism. The German passion for order can on occasion throw up the sternest anarchist, devoted to the destruction of a regime.

I was not one of that breed, and swiftly drifted away in the post-war years. Apart from initial approaches, my 'godparents' left me alone. The OSS, having established that I was a minor cog in a self-regulating Left-wing movement, paid me no more attention. I returned to the Merchant Marine, working on numerous Dutch and German ships.

All the while I kept in infrequent touch with Die Wasserkante comrades to discover if they had heard anything of Oskar von Niedermayer. He remained for me the *beau idéal* of manhood and service to a cause greater than himself. Had he ordered me to stick with Die Wasserkante I do not see how I could have refused.

Niedermayer had gone over to the Russians. Of that we had no doubt. Held in custody just South of Berlin in the last hours of hostilities, he had informed captive fellow-officers he was 'going East'.

The years passed, and no word came from him or about him. I was not unduly concerned, because Niedermayer was naturally a man of mystery: working against the British secretly in Persia and Afghanistan during the First World War; clandestinely helping the Reichswehr to train in Soviet Russia during the twenties; directing an underground against the Nazis in the thirties and forties. It was perfectly understandable if he should now be helping the world cause of communism where his abilities and experience would prove of most use — perhaps guiding the Chinese communists in their military offensives against Chiang Kai-shek's nationalists.

I had no means of knowing that Oskar, Ritter von Niedermayer, had died in a Soviet prison in Vladimir, east of Moscow, in 1948. Thirty years were to go by before his family received confirmation of his death.

I wonder if Niedermayer enjoyed the irony of being imprisoned by Hitler for not being a Nazi and by Stalin for being too much of a communist? For Niedermayer's crime was that he had been a friend of Leon Trotsky, the first political chief of the Red Army, and Stalin's sworn foe. Trotsky, the apostle of continuing revolution, was a far more important figure than Stalin in Niedermayer's early days. He was also a much more colourful figure, stimulating and ebullient, than the dour, sullen, suspicious Joseph Stalin.

To Stalin any communist tainted with Western cosmopolitanism, let alone friendship with the 'Jew Trotsky', was a menace. He would remember the old days; he would start questioning the policies of the man who had arranged for Trotsky's murder in 1940. German communists who would click their jackboots to the new Russian Order were acceptable — even necessary and desirable. But those with the faintest connections with Trotsky . . .

I do not know to this day whether Niedermayer died a natural death or was helped on his way. He would have been sixty-two in 1948. He was, when I last saw him in the spring of 1945, fit, lean and healthy.

Each year I expected him to reappear, and in case he should choose to return to his native Bavaria, I refrained from publishing anything about him or his activities with Die Wasserkante lest — as said in the note at the beginning of this book — it affected his position in West Germany.

The notes I had written up in 1945 and 1946 remained in a drawer in my home town of Zutphen. I married a happy Irish girl in 1958 and finally settled in England, and it was she who suggested I should look out my old papers and find out what had happened to Oskar von Niedermayer. So I wrote to the Niedermayer family in Munich and received from Frau Thilde Niedermayer — his brother's widow — a letter dated 19 November, 1978.

In the course of it she wrote:

> The brother of my deceased husband, Oskar von
> Niedermayer, went from Torgau[1] to Moscow as a prisoner
> of war; later, when already seriously ill, he was taken to
> Vladimir, which is about 60 km from Moscow. There he
> died on September 25, 1948. It took us several years to
> have definite news about his fate. My sister-in-law, Berta
> von Niedermayer, died in April 1954.

In a letter four weeks later Frau Thilde wrote:

> It is not correct that my brother-in-law had been kidnapped
> by the Soviets. As far as I remember prisoners of war in
> the Torgau area were liberated by the US Army. My
> brother-in-law voluntarily gave himself up to the Soviets as
> he was perfectly sure he would be handed over to the
> Soviets sooner or later by the Americans. Apparently this
> had been his most serious mistake. This mistake might be
> understandable from the point of view of my
> brother-in-law and also for the following reasons:
>   From 1923 he had spent (with the full approval of the
> Soviet Government and military authorities) 10 years in
> Moscow. Having made the acquaintance of a number of
> prominent personalities and having made some friends
> among them in these years, he may have supposed that his
> case might find fair judgment. This was an error. Without
> any justification at all he was charged with espionage and
> sentenced to 25 years imprisonment. Please understand
> this. He has not deserved this fate.

Clearly Frau Thilde knew little or nothing about her late bro-
ther-in-law's connection with the communist underground in
Germany.

But Niedermayer's conviction that the Americans would hand
him over to the Russians — of which the family learned from
released German prisoners-of-war who had known Niedermayer in Vladimir — strongly suggests that Niedermayer was
sure the Americans would stumble on his political past and dispatch him to his political masters. He paid with his life for his
'serious mistake' in going over to the Russians, for the Americans
would undoubtedly have permitted him to remain in the West.

This confirmation of Niedermayer's tragic end made me
resolve to tell the story of Die Wasserkante and the secret of
Torgau. My wife has encouraged me in this venture, and so the

---

[1] Actually he had been moved some kilometres from Torgau.

notes which had been gathering dust for three decades were brought into the light.

In telling my story I, the last survivor of Torgau, have discharged my debt to the forgotten men of Festung Zinna, who so nearly changed the course of history.

Index